Ontology of Construction explores theories of construction in modern architecture, with particular focus on the relationship between nihilism of technology and architecture. Providing a historical context for the concept of "making," the essays collected in this volume articulate the implications of technology in works by such architects as Le Corbusier, Frank Lloyd Wright, Adolf Loos, and Mies van der Rohe. They also offer an interpretation of Gottfried Semper's discourse on the tectonic and the relationship between architecture and other crafts. Emphasizing "fabrication" as a critical theme for contemporary architectural theory and practice, *Ontology of Construction* is a provocative contribution to the current debate in these areas.

T0345815

ONTOLOGY OF CONSTRUCTION

Ontology of Construction

On Nihilism of Technology in Theories
of Modern Architecture

GEVORK HARTOONIAN

CAMBRIDGE
UNIVERSITY PRESS

CAMBRIDGE UNIVERSITY PRESS

Cambridge, New York, Melbourne, Madrid, Cape Town,
Singapore, São Paulo, Delhi, Tokyo, Mexico City

Cambridge University Press
The Edinburgh Building, Cambridge CB2 8RU, UK

Published in the United States of America by
Cambridge University Press, New York

www.cambridge.org
Information on this title: www.cambridge.org/9780521586450

© Cambridge University Press 1994

First published 1994
First paperback edition 1997

A catalogue record for this publication is available from the British Library

ISBN 978-0-521-58645-0 Paperback

To My Mother

CONTENTS

List of Illustrations   *page* IX

Foreword by Kenneth Frampton   XI

Acknowledgments   XVII

Introduction   I

1 Montage: Recoding the Tectonic   5

2 Architecture and the Question of Technology:
   Two Positions and the "Other"   29

3 Adolf Loos: The Awakening Moments of
   Tradition in Modern Architecture   43

4 Métier: Frank Lloyd Wright's Tradition
   of Dwelling   56

5 Mies van der Rohe: The Genealogy of
   Column and Wall   68

6 Construction of the Not Yet Construed   81

Notes   91

Index   111

ILLUSTRATIONS

1 Leon Battista Alberti, Palazzo Rucellai,
Florence, 1446–51   *page* 8

2 The hut on display at the Great Exhibition,
London, 1851   21

3 Egyptian capital with lotus flower inserts
and Persian capital with volutes imitating
Assyrian hollow-body construction   25

4 Knots   25

5 Signet of the Staatliche Bauhaus, from 1919
to 1921   31

6 Signet of the Staatliche Bauhaus, after a design
by Oskar Schlemmer, 1922   31

7 Adolf Loos, Looshaus, Michaelerplatz, Vienna,
1909–11, overall view   45

8 Adolf Loos, Looshaus, Michaelerplatz, Vienna,
1909–11, plan   47

9 A contemporary cartoon of the Looshaus   48

10 A 1911 cartoon of the Looshaus facade   48

11 Adolf Loos, Steiner House, Vienna, 1910   49

12 Baldassare Peruzzi, Villa Farnesina,
Rome, 1508–10   51

13 Karl Friedrich Schinkel, Urban
Residence project   51

14 Frank Lloyd Wright, Ward Willits House,
Highland Park, Illinois, 1900   59

15 Frank Lloyd Wright, Robie House,
Chicago, 1909   60

16 Bruce Price, Kent House, Tuxedo Park,
New York, 1885–6   61

ILLUSTRATIONS   17 Frank Lloyd Wright, Martin House, Buffalo,
                     New York, 1904, plan   62

                 18 Frank Lloyd Wright, Winslow House, River
                     Forest, Illinois, 1893, front and rear views   63

                 19 Frank Lloyd Wright, Unity Temple, Oak
                     Park, Illinois, 1906, plan and street view   65

                 20 Mies van der Rohe, Concrete Country House
                     project, 1923   71

                 21 Mies van der Rohe, Brick Country House
                     project, 1923–4, plan and perspective   71

                 22 Mies van der Rohe, Barcelona Pavilion,
                     1928, plan   72

                 23 Mies van der Rohe, Tugendhat House, Brno,
                     1928–30, plan of ground floor   74

                 24 Mies van der Rohe, Barcelona Pavilion, 1928   75

                 25 50 × 50 House project, 1950–1   77

                 26 Mies van der Rohe, Illinois Institute of
                     Technology campus, Chicago, 1942, detail   79

                 27 Marc-Antoine Laugier, cover page for *Essai
                     sur l'architecture* (Paris, 1755)   83

FOREWORD

As the title of this collection implies, the primary theme that
these essays address is the searching and difficult question of
how the reality of the man-made environment can be structured, both ethically and rationally, in a highly operational
and secularized technoscientific age. As the author is prompt
to point out, this question is neither new nor singular and has
in fact been continuously rising in the modern consciousness
since the end of the eighteenth century. As he shows, following the lead of the Frankfurt school, this aporia has been
brought about by the triumph of global technology and its
penetration of every aspect of the life-world. While the English Pre-Raphaelite and Arts and Crafts intellectuals of the
mid-nineteenth century – among them, A. W. N. Pugin, John
Ruskin, and William Morris – were the first to react against
the erosion of both tradition and faith under the impact of the
Industrial Revolution, the deeper cultural consequences of
this technological transformation were not adequately articulated until the exceptionally perceptive writings of the German architect and cultural theorist Gottfried Semper – above
all, his *Science, Industry and Art* and his *Four Elements of Architecture,* both published in 1852. While the former first
posed, without a trace of sentiment, the still extant question
concerning the evident devaluation of traditional craft-based
culture through the advent of industrial reproduction and
mass consumption, with all the simulations and substitutions
that this inevitably entails – as Semper put it, "How will
time or science bring law and order into this thoroughly con-
fused state of affairs?" – the latter, with its focus upon a Caribbean hut exhibited in the Great Exhibition of 1851,
assumed for the first time what one may call the ethno-
graphic Archimedean point that was returned to repeatedly
by critical intellectuals throughout the succeeding century.

This anthropological interest in remote preindustrial civilizations and even in pre-agricultural nomadic cultures will serve spontaneously as a compensatory reference for some future self-realization of the species located outside the nightmare of history, beyond that which Walter Benjamin once characterized as the "storm of progress."

This interest in the archaic, remote from the bourgeois world, has taken on distinctly different guises in different hands. Despite these variations, however, a discernible thread runs through the thought of a number of figures as the twentieth century unfolds, ranging from architects as diverse as Frank Lloyd Wright, Adolf Loos, Le Corbusier, and Mies van der Rohe to generic intellectuals as diffuse in their ideological affinities as Benjamin, Georg Simmel, Theodor Adorno, and Martin Heidegger, as well as the much less renowned Jesuit philosopher Romano Guardini, who exercised such a decisive influence on the work and thought of Mies. The scope of this critical intelligentsia widened after the Second World War to include existentialist thinkers such as Jean-Paul Sartre and later the French poststructuralist philosophers Michel Foucault and Jean Baudrillard and, last but not least, the Italian philosopher Gianni Vattimo, whose advocacy of "weak thought" seems to be the aspirational light, so to speak, at the end of Hartoonian's tunnel. While the author discusses all of these figures, along with many others too numerous to mention here, the architects Gottfried Semper and Adolf Loos come to the fore as the two figures that carry, as it were, the main burden of his argument – the former for his general theory of tectonic culture and the latter for the Kraussian skepticism that he brings to the entire enterprise.

Semper is undeniably important for his fundamental break with the classical Vitruvian triad, *utilitas, firmitas,* and *venustas,* and for his formulation of an aformal, sociocultural theory – his *Four Elements of Architecture* comprising the archaic components of *earthwork, hearth, roofwork,* and *screen wall.* The woven, non-load-bearing character of this last led Semper back through multiple examples of nomadic culture to the primacy of textile production and to the cladding of both men and built-form (*Bekleidung*) and, finally, to the fundamental nexus of the knot as the primordial joint upon which the cosmological tectonic art of construction must be ultimately based. For Semper, the structural symbolic essence of tectonics was necessarily closer to the cosmological ritualistic arts of music and dance than to the figurative arts of painting and sculpture, and this distinction would no doubt inspire Loos's subsequent discrimination between the building tasks of the life-world and the commemorative role of architecture in its monumental aspect – the tomb and the monument.

For Loos, the technological secularization of culture entailed, among other things, a repudiation of the Christian Gothic tradition, and this had the effect of distancing him from the European structuralist protomodern line in all its guises from Eugène Viollet-le-Duc to Antonio Gaudi. Although he would adopt the American Arts and Crafts, Queen Anne manner in many of his domestic interiors, as the liberal-progressive Anglo-American mode, he nonetheless looked back to Schinkel and neoclassic form for architecture at its most honorific. Distanced to an equal degree from both historicism and avant-gardism and preoccupied as Semper had been by the need to transform traditional paradigms in light of the new productive means, Loos attempted the acrobatic feat of sustaining tradition while simultaneously embracing the inevitable and seemingly liberating thrust of technology. This dichotomous attitude is evident from one of his ironic aphorisms, in which he wrote, "There is no point in inventing anything unless it is an improvement," a sentiment that is surely equally applicable to both tradition and technology.

Loos's delicate parody of the Richardsonian domestic manner, replete with false Tudor beams and wainscoting, would, as Hartoonian remarks, citing Vattimo, preserve tradition by undermining its content, with the result that these *Gemutlich* interiors are both reassuring and subtly subversive. They speak of Georg Simmel's alienating metropolis in the context of which they were merely to function as some kind of reassuring mise-en-scène. Their value-free outer walls find an appropriately silent expression in Loos's blank, monochromatic facades pierced by square windows and stripped of all ornament. Influenced by Semper's *Bekleidung* thesis, Loos attempted to impose an ethical nihilism on the already schizophrenic, mechanized metropolis wherein things would be dressed or undressed according to the required pathos of their action setting. Thus, the house would be clad within but unclad without, where everything had already been reduced to the abstractions of capitalist speculation, to which Loos responded with the cryptic declaration that revealed the critical Kraussian stance underlying his work. His famous slogan "The house is conservative and the work of art is revolutionary" already hints at the fact that his work has to be seen as a mixture of both. In the main, the only exception to his nihilistic blank syntax was either the false vernacular, which he reserved for his vacation houses, set in open countryside, or the classical monumentality of the occasional public institution.

Hartoonian remarks with exceptional clairvoyance that Frank Lloyd Wright, subject to different circumstances, met the needs of an alienated, migrant, middle class with a totally different strategy:

From 1893 to 1910, Wright set down a metaphoric language known as Prairie architecture. What distinguishes this period from the rest of Wright's career is the attempt he makes to restate tradition by new means and materials. Unlike architects from the Arts and Crafts movement, he never yearned for the cottage. . . . In contrast to classical architecture, in Wright's plan, the cross axis neither sustains frontality nor initiates a symmetrical order. In the Ward Willets house, Wright summons the basic sensation of place, as if a nomad were experiencing it. In this context, the cross axis is the abstract representation of the natural existence of the earth, a device for orientation, settlement, and departure. . . . In almost every plan, the center is given over to the hearth, the fireplace, where the comfort attained through its warmth stimulates a temporary feeling of settlement.

Looking back across the history of modernity, Hartoonian conceives of montage as the quintessentially late modern cultural strategy, one that is as disjunctive in film as it is conjunctive in architecture and also, paradoxically, vice versa. He sees the act of montage as the one mediatory agent whereby tradition may be reinterpreted and hence *recollected* in face of the operational inroads and transformations wrought by technology. In the process of evolving that which Hartoonian identifies as the "ontology of the present," montage proceeds as much by concealing as by revealing, as in the work of Mies van der Rohe, say, or even more perhaps in the dialectic of junction and disjunction in the work of the Italian architect Carlo Scarpa.

Scarpa's work brings to light all the ambiguity that lies within the word "fabrication," which signifies not only the act of making but also the more negative connotation indicating the creation of an artifice bordering on falsehood. It is an architecture of revetment par excellence, in which what is revealed reciprocally presupposes a certain masking by definition. This in itself is hardly new, but what is unique in Scarpa's production is the way in which this expressive play between exotic revetment, on the one hand, and the naked

materiality, on the other, is often combined with an exces-
sively rhetorical elaboration of the joint or seam between
them. Scarpa thereby engenders a complex discourse in his
work in which structure and ornament are part and parcel of
the same movement. According to Hartoonian, both of these
attributes are etymologically inscribed in the Greek word
kosmos, signifying both universe and decoration, a synthesis
that is echoed today in such common words as "cosmos" and
"cosmetic." As Hartoonian puts it (and here, he seems to be
alluding to Scarpa):

> Traditionally, the symbolic function of architecture was an at-
> tribute of its monumentality, signifying by its classical language a
> definitive universality. . . . And yet "emptied" of its representa-
> tional connotations, a monument is an ornament par excellence,
> the significance of which rests not in the fixation of a set of values,
> but in pointing to the occurrence of an event that forms a back-
> ground for our collective experience (Semper's artifice?) generating
> a multiplicity of interpretation.

Value, event, background, and collective experience are
terms that suggest the necessary consummation of architecture through social ritual and life experience – in other
words, a programmatic articulation of built-form bordering
on the theatrical, that is, an open-ended expressivity to which
Scarpa seems to have been particularly dedicated. Thus, the
"construction of the not yet construed" would appear to pre-
suppose a creativity that is grounded in a perpetual state of
postponement, a kind of deliberately unfinished technostatic
event that Ernst Bloch would elsewhere characterize more
generally as a *projected hope.* This is where Hartoonian leaves
us in his rereading of the evolution of architectural modernity
in terms of both theory and practice. It is a precise, informed,
but open-ended rereading that demands in itself to be constantly reread and reinterpreted. In this sense it is by definition an unfinished work, a didactic "not yet" that prompts
further reflection on what could one day still prove to be a
new form of ethical practice.

KENNETH FRAMPTON

ACKNOWLEDGMENTS

I am writing these lines at a moment of my existence when the delight of publishing my first book and an ongoing struggle for identity and recognition have come together to impress upon me one more time that I am nothing but a being thrown into the world. Among friends who have borne my anxieties, I especially thank Kenneth Frampton, from whom I have learned to think of the poetics of construction, though I realize more than ever how far I remain from what he can do and has done for the craft of architecture. I am also thankful for his friendship and those moments of intellectual exchange that have profited me enormously. I am grateful to Harry Francis Mallgrave for concrete and constructive comments. I am also thankful for David Leatherbarrow's critical comments and advice. The title of the final chapter, "Construction of the Not Yet Construed," speaks for my debt to Marco Frascari's discourse, and I express my thanks for his counsel and encouragement throughout my academic work. I am indebted to Peggy Irish for her careful editing of an early draft. My thanks go to Beatrice Rehl at Cambridge University Press, whose effort in publishing this book was enormous. Finally, I am conscious of how much I have profited from the intellectual exchange with my friends and colleagues at the University of Pennsylvania.

INTRODUCTION

The object of this work is to explore the process of secularization, or demythification, of the concept of construction in
architecture. Architectural treatises discuss construction extensively, yet its significance has been framed by the metaphysical context of *techne,* grounding a concept of "making"
that conforms with the implacable and coherent system of
aesthetic values and technical norms discussed in humanist
discourse. Even Marc-Antoine Laugier's challenge to Vitruvius had to remain in the realm of theory: Laugier's hut could
have achieved its architectonic form only by melding its normative discourse with the idea of *techne,* thus representing the
homology between the realm of values and the empirical aspects of construction.

Gottfried Semper's ideas on the tectonic suggest a breach
between meaning and construction. Semper radicalized the
question concerning the origin of architecture to the point
that the anthropocentric narrative of architecture was replaced by a discourse whose formative themes rest in four
separate industries. This was an important step in breaking
down the coherent totality and linear progression of humanist discourse anticipating montage: a mode of thinking and
making that weakens the metaphysical context of both *techne*
and the tectonic and that stresses the automization of value
and experience.

The theme of construction does not occupy a formative
place in current architectural discourse. Part of the reason for
this is that most current theories tend to criticize some aspects of modernity and its subsequent themes and concepts,
which evolved around the mid-nineteenth century. The
mechanization of production and the emergence of industrial
materials and techniques made it possible to read Gothic ar-

I

chitecture in light of Laugier's positivistic understanding of architectural production. The nineteenth century's esteem for eclectic style reflected a state of architectural thinking in which the loss of the classical language was felt to be inevitable, while no alternative was yet available. This historical delay was epitomized, for instance, by the different ways Victor Horta and Frank Furness articulated the steel column or, later, the ways in which Le Corbusier abstracted it. The gap between what was past and what was yet to appear marked a definite end to the concept of *techne,* whose classical language was already distilled, leaving room for architects to conceive form (geometry) as an expressive element.

Techne is the Greek word for technology; it means "the art of making." Martin Heidegger defines *techne* as both "poetic and revealing." In this seeming paradox, *techne* not only designates tools and fabrication; it primarily signifies their place in the world of values. This reading of the word was suggested in Vitruvius's *De Architectura.* Architecture, Vitruvius contends, achieves unity when nothing can be added to or taken away from it: thus, the three-part compositional norm carried out in every classical artifact is not only a pure aesthetic category but also a way of seeing and constructing.

Renaissance architects charged the word *techne* with connotations related to the Christian duality between divine and earthly life. Leon Battista Alberti's discourse on lineaments comes to mind in relation to this. For him, design and construction were two separate but interrelated issues: construction embodied all those technical arts needed to carry out the work, while design, or lineaments, preceded construction and embodied the correct and precise outline of the design as it was made up of lines and angles.

Alberti's distinction anticipated the contemporary schism between theory and practice; the duality of design and construction has prevailed in modern discourse as well. Yet the differences between the nineteenth-century reading of that duality and today's should be addressed. Neither John Ruskin nor Viollet-le-Duc, for example, could help but attempt to reconcile Laugier's empirical interpretation of the word "construction" with the recurrent theme of ornament or style. Ruskin's thought on the relationship between ornament and structure and Viollet-le-Duc's insistence that the appearance of a building should express its construction are in fact two different expressions of the same idea. Since that time, design has been considered the poetic expression of an ideal architecture. In order to utilize industrial materials and techniques, nineteenth-century architects had no choice but to change their classificatory mode.

This discursive transformation is important for understanding Gottfried Semper's thought on the tectonic. There are two points in Semper's definition of the tectonic that prompt consideration of his discourse transcending humanist culture. First, in opposition to the traditional classification of architecture with the representational arts, Semper considered the tectonic to be a cosmic art, analogous to music and dance. Second, in criticizing the historicism and aestheticism of his time, Semper associated the tectonic with other constructive artifacts, primarily with four industries: ceramics, carpentry, masonry, and textiles. From this point of view, architectural production became entangled with the existential aspects of life.

The importance of montage in current architectural discourse stems from Semper's thought: the idea that the act of making a place evolved out of techniques developed in other industries. Montage is not only a mode of making shared by the production process of various cultural artifacts; it also embodies the contemporary experience of fragmentation. The mechanization of reproduction has made it impossible to transfer tradition, including the craft of architecture, without subjecting it to the process of secularization that has supplanted the Christian idea of redemption with the idea of progress. Montage permits a discourse through which it is possible to deprive the metaphysical content of the duality between construction and representation. It reveals its tectonic form in the "dis-joint," a weak form that distances sign from signifier. The gap thus opened between sign and signifier provides the thematic mode for recoding the tectonic as the construction of a purposeful space.

The essays collected in this volume explore the theme of the secularization of construction through the thoughts and work of contemporary architects sensitive to the subject. The essays are not ordered chronologically. In fact, Chapter 1 was written most recently. Other chapters were originally prepared for conferences or journals and were revised for this volume. Each chapter stands independently, but my concentration on technology, construction, and materials will be obvious. And my debt to Gianni Vattimo will be evident in my advocation of the case for secularization.

The theme of construction and its poetic implications for architecture have been my interest for many years. Intrigued by Mies van der Rohe's architecture and Semper's oeuvre, I could not help but pursue the question of technology beyond its empirical dimension. Yet I have not directly involved myself with the matters concerning the metaphysics of technology; still, the reader will be able to follow the implications of philosophy and criticism for architecture, a subject clearly important for my own academic and professional work.

The merit of this book is implied in the title of its final chapter, "Construction of the Not Yet Construed": these essays disclose an architectural discourse that in Blochian manner is yet to come. This I believe to be the positive fruit of the nihilism of technology and the process of secularization, that is, the eternal return of the same in different formal guises. The final chapter responds to this last point by recalling Adolf Loos's position in the history of contemporary architecture. My intention is not to apotheosize him; but bearing in mind the experience of modern discourse on utopia, we might read the postmodern condition of architecture in light of Loos's anticipation of the "death" of architecture, its relegation to the tomb and monument. In fact, it is necessary to go beyond Loos, to construe the monument not as an architectonic representation of power or a "historical" event, but as the event itself: an act of construction and gathering whose architecture would be associated with the realm of values through recollection.

CHAPTER 1

MONTAGE

Recoding the Tectonic

TECHNE: THE POETICS OF CLASSICAL WISDOM

The absence of "structural utility" as a theme in the architectural discourse of classicism was caused by an ontological relationship between meaning and work. The legacy of Galileo's observations and of Cartesian doubt provided motivation for the epistemological rupture with classical thought. The implications for architecture included a positivistic concept of beauty and a new understanding of the classical order. The concept of fabrication,¹ in which the process of building became a determinant of the cultural values of the final product, was another important result. All three helped to dissolve the classical understanding of the relationship between style and construction that was signified by the word *techne.*

The last decades of the seventeenth century marked the end of the traditional guilds in Paris. They were replaced by the academies and by the institution of the Corps des Ponts et Chaussées. This was the first step toward modification of the classical discourse of architecture. Later, in 1756, the replacement of the Corps des Ponts et Chaussées with the Ecole des Ponts et Chaussées initiated the separation of the two disciplines of engineering and architecture.

These historical events had a great impact upon architectural knowledge: they confirmed the schism between mechanical and liberal arts already realized by Filipo Brunelleschi's work on the dome of Santa Maria del Fiore. Brunelleschi conceived a dome beyond the horizon of existing techniques and skills. According to Giulio Argan, "A sharp differentiation thus came about between ideative techniques – activities of thinking and translation into precise projects – and the work of execution, whose sole task was to put such plans into effect was so determined."² It was a significant step toward the contemporary understanding of the separation of design from construction activity.

In line with eighteenth-century developments in the mechanical sciences, the nineteenth century's moral functionalists and their modernist successors highly valued machines and industrial achievements and conceived of architectural production as a process of design and building in which technology was the determinant. Mirroring the course of the production line, the status of architecture was either reduced to that of a utensil, as was the case in the Werkbund and Bauhaus schools, or the field was wrongly assumed by some disciples of the Russian Constructivists to be equivalent to engineering. In both approaches, "structural utility" was conceived of as instrumental. Losing their metaphoric significance, column, beam, and wall were reduced to the level of structural techniques serving expressive intentions. Indeed, technology in modern architecture is particularized by continual fluctuation between two extremes – concealment and exposure – of "structural utility." In either case, the relationship between style and construction is problematic.

In light of the current revisions to, and elaborations on, modernist thought, it could be argued that the main effort of modern architecture has been directed at freeing itself from the classical language of architecture.[3] The syntax of the classical language of architecture derives from a body of rules and principles that are in conformity with concepts of reason and divine revelation. A reading of Vitruvius's and Andrea Palladio's treatises on architecture might convince a reader that an instrumental view of structural techniques was critical to the breaking away of modernism from the architectural discourse on classicism.

One important aspect of classical thought was its ontological understanding of work. In the classical discourse of architecture, work was conceptualized as the unity of thinking and doing. Congruity between theory and practice, or thinking and doing, was of such importance to the classical knowledge of architecture that Vitruvius dedicated his first book to this subject. In *De Architectura* we read: "In all matters, but particularly in architecture, there are these two points: the thing signified, and that which gives it its significance. That which is signified is the subject of which we may be speaking; and that which gives significance is a demonstration on scientific principles."[4] This statement suggests that, in classical thought, architecture was viewed as a discipline in itself which, like other natural phenomena, possessed a subject matter and a body of principles as its raison d'être. According to Vitruvius, an architect must be aware not only of history, which provides a rich repository of architectural typologies, but also of the physical rules governing materials. I would suggest that the Vitruvian trinity is not a theoretical abstraction on the aesthetic function of architecture. Rather, *venustas, utilitas,* and *firmitas* are the formative themes of an architectural knowledge in which style is integrated with the rules of gravity and the property of materials. In fact, they provide a conceptual means of transmuting the contingent reality of construction, elevating building into architecture. Yet the transformation of a hut into a temple does not result from a mimetic act. Vitruvius speaks of rituals, of the names of kings and localities as the mythopoetic dimension of the Greek orders.[5]

Renaissance architects read Vitruvius in light of Leon Battista Alberti's discourse in *De re aedificatoria.* It is true that Brunelleschi set down the practical side of the separation of the architect from the workman, but it was left to Alberti to formulate the theoretical ground of this historical development. In his discourse on lineaments, Alberti suggested that the "whole matter of building is composed of lineaments and structure." And he continued, the purpose of lineaments "lies in finding the correct, infallible way of joining and fitting together those lines and angles which define and enclose the surfaces of the building."[6] A distinction between structure and appearance remains problematic for Western architecture. One might see in Alberti's definition of lineaments some traits of what, later, Semper would call "clothing." Nevertheless, this kind of analogy does not convey the abstract content of Alberti's ideas on lineaments. Semper's discourse suggests that the tectonic evolves through the structural needs of a building and its clothing, while lineaments remain independent of structure and have nothing to do with materials. They also remain indifferent to purpose and form. Disregarding material and structure, lineaments become the sole content of design, "the precise and correct outline, conceived in the mind, made up of lines and angles, and perfected in the learned intellect and imagination."[7] Alberti's design for Palazzo Rucellai represents the fundamental character of his thoughts on lineaments (Figure 1). The lines separating columns from the wall, the curves of the windows' arches, and finally the horizontal and vertical bands of the facade of Palazzo Rucellai seem to be cut out of cardboard and pasted over the structure. Nothing confirms the separa-

Figure 1. Leon Battista
Alberti, Palazzo Rucellai,
Florence, 1446–51. From
Christian Norberg-Schulz,
*Meaning in Western
Architecture* (New York:
Rizzoli International
Publications, 1980).

tion of lineaments from structure better than the different articulation of the first floor of this building from the upper
ones. But such an abstract concept of the difference between
the lines, distracting the eye of the viewer from the structure
of the building, affirms the specificity of Renaissance culture,
where every artifact was seen in light of what Jean Baudrillard calls the "first-order" of simulacrum; a counterfeit in
which the natural, that is, structure, lives alongside the false,
that is, the appearance.[8]

The ontological duality between the body and matter
could be further explored by examining the congruity of the
body of Christ and the crucifix. In making this analogy, the
cross, which is an important sacred symbol in Christian culture, maintains a critical place in the traditional discourse of
construction. Its significance for architecture is twofold.
First, it designates a space between the body and matter that
could be related to the chiasm between construction and ornament. In addition to its metaphorical reference to suffering, the body of Christ may also be seen as an ornament
added to the crucifix. Understanding the addition in mean-

ing that causes the figure of Christ both to symbolize suffering and to act as an ornament greatly enhances our comprehension of the process of secularization that occurred in construction. If one considers Alberti's assertion that ornament, "rather than being inherent,"[9] is a supplement that complements beauty, then it makes sense for us moderns to think of the removal of both pain and any ornamental addition to the body of the building. Such surgical intention blossoms in Adolf Loos's polemical claim that "ornament is a crime." Not only does Loos's statement disclose his dislike of Viennese Secessionist tendencies; more important, it can be read as an affirmative reflection on the general process of cultural secularization, whose genealogy could be located in the very realization of the cross itself. According to Elaine Scarry, the cross not only marks the end of the view that God is the sole maker, but initiates a total change in the construct of tools and realization of material culture.[10] I would argue that cultural demythification also marks a nihilistic discourse on construction. Here the word "nihilism" signifies the distance of civilization from the realm of the sacred, as manifested in every act of cultural production. It is a historical process of desecration through which "all that is solid melts into air."[11] But beyond the negative connotation of Karl Marx's statement, one might point out an affirmative aspect as well. Marx's writing assumes that sentience and imagination are collectively expressed in our material world:

[On the one hand,] the "system of production" is a materialization of the imagination's own activity of "making" (just as in the older writings the Primary Artifact, God, is itself the objectification of the human power of "creating" with all the ethical requirements and complications of that power brought fully into view). On the other hand, it is an artful extension of the metabolic and genetic secrets of the human body.[12]

One might argue that we need to have second thoughts in regard to a concept of construction that, in lieu of the early process of mechanization, would take refuge in the moral values of the guild system (as did the Arts and Crafts movement) or else would invent grand narratives speculating on the redemptive forces of technology. This proposition is suggestive if we place the nihilistic aspect of the separation of design from structure and the question concerning ornament in the context of an affirmative reading of Western cultural discourse, which was stigmatized not only in Marx but in Friedrich Nietzsche as well.

The second import of the cross is its typological connotation. Renaissance cultural discourse was not in a position to
see this implication of the cross. How is it possible to depart
from the realm of the sacred if culture is understood within
the metaphysics of resemblance? Even the Renaissance reinterpretation of Virtruvius's ideal man would not have been
possible without imposing the idea of "the procreator of
square, circles and the like, and the hermetic model and
source of architectural form."[13] One can trace the formal expression of the cross in the Renaissance obsession with the interplay of the circle and the square, finding its architectural
language in Francesco di Giorgio's churches and Palladio's
villas. In his preface to *The Four Books of Architecture,* Palladio
emphasized the typological significance of *techne.*[14] In his observations on Greek and Roman architecture, he found everything in conformity with reason and beautiful proportion.
Indeed, these findings became the motto of Palladio's discourse on architecture: "I know therefore nothing that can be
done more contrary to natural reason." In support of his argument, Palladio refers to the necessity of integrating reason
with art: "Although variety and new things may please everyone, yet they ought not to be done to the precepts of art,
and contrary to that which reason dictates."[15] Is not Palladio
suggesting that in classical thought *techne* was understood as
the logos of making? Certain aspects of this logos are suggestive of the kind of association I am intending to make between construction and type. We read in Arendt that as the
dominant mode of fabrication in the age of premechaniza-
tion, craftsmanship integrated labor with the final products
of labor. And work was planned and executed by craftspeople who had an image of the product in mind from the start.
Furthermore, contemplation was "considered to be an inherent element in fabrication as well, inasmuch as the work of
the craftsman was guided by the idea, the model beheld by
him before it had ended."[16] In other words, the technique of
making an artifact could not be conceived of as separate from
the image of the object itself. It would, then, be possible to
say that work was performed by means of commonly understood cultural typologies.

In pursuing such a canon, one might assume that order is
the architectonic figuration of column and beam that has
evolved through the historical development of different architectural types. According to Vitruvius, a theater "would
not be subject to the same rules of symmetry and proportion
which I presented in the case of sanctuaries; for the dignity

which ought to be their quality in temples of the gods is one thing, but their elegance in colonnades and other public works is quite another." Later he advises his readers: "Let the modular proportion of the rest of the work be carried out as written in the fourth book in the case of temple."[17] Thus, we can state that Vitruvius's treatise is a theoretical formulation of the ontological relationship between architectural typology and its logos of making. In classical texts on architecture, notions such as the "styles of walls," the "order of columns," and the "nature of materials" are utilized not with regard to their empirical characteristics, but as architectonic elements. The presence of order as a theme in the classical discourse of architecture signifies the transition of column and beam from their load-bearing imperatives into stylistic representation. In this regard, Vitruvius believed that the transformation of a hut into a temple reveals a historical move from undefined concepts to definite rules of symmetry.[18]

Accordingly, we can state that *techne,* in the classical concept of work, did not signify a means, but the unity of means and end. Tools, materials, and knowledge of their use were "in the service of efforts to mirror realities more perfectly."[19] Such a concept of work is indicative of the unique discourse of art and science. In the Renaissance, according to Agnes Heller, art and science provided an intersubjective mode of learning in which the relation between man, tool, and nature was ontological. A major implication of Heller's argument is that such unification was a mirror of a greater unity, the unity between man and universe. In emphasizing this view, Michel Foucault maintains that resemblance and similitude were the two major forms of knowledge in the Renaissance. According to him, "To search for the law governing signs is to discover the signs that are alike."[20] In architecture, this means that architectural elements might have operated metaphorically: in the classical world of resemblance, column and wall were not identical to their load-bearing efficiency. Rather, these structural elements functioned as signs understood by their resemblance to nature and the human body. Thus, in comprehending the relationship between different phenomena through resemblance, classical architects' conceptualizations of the different functions of architectural elements were integrated with their technical knowledge.

An understanding of *techne* as the logos of making is critical to the plan, sectional organization, and aesthetic function of Palladian architecture. For the design of villas, Palladio recommends:

The rooms ought to be distributed on each side of the entry and hall, and it is to be observed that those on the right correspond with those on the left, so that the fabric may be the same in one place as in the other, and that the walls may equally bear the burden of the roof; because if the rooms are made large in one part, and small in the other, the latter will be more fit to resist the weight, by reason of the nearness of the walls, and the former more weak, which will produce in time very great inconveniences, and ruin the whole work.[21]

Therefore, we can postulate that symmetry, when used as the organizing principle of Palladian villas, was not merely an aesthetic device. Motivated by the proportions of the human body and cosmic order, symmetry in Palladian architecture signified the integration of beauty with rules of fabrication. For Palladio, the logos of the plan also motivated the facade and sectional organization:

The windows on the right hand ought to correspond to those on the left, and those above directly over them that are below; and those likewise ought to be directly over another, that the void may be over the void, and the solid upon solid, and all face one another, so that standing at one end of the house one may see to the other, which affords both beauty and cool air in summer, besides other convenience.[22]

In such an understanding of architecture, the appropriate use of fascia and cornice as detailing devices covered the proportional rise of a wall and signified "arms holding the two sides of a wall."[23] In the discourses of Palladio and Vitruvius, *techne* unfolds an ontological relationship between work and meaning that achieves its architectonic expression in Vitruvius's belief that the total unity of architecture was secured when nothing could be added or taken away from it, meaning that the three-part compositional norm present in every classical artifact is not only a pure aesthetic category, but a way of seeing and constructing.[24]

Classical thought was undermined by the consecutive processes of secularization that have characterized the modern age. Humanity's perception of the world was transformed by the invention of the telescope, by Galileo's observations, and by a shift of interest toward the life processes of physical nature.[25] An interest in logic and an analytical approach to natural and cultural phenomena became the basic characteristics of the modern age. Losing its metaphorical essence in the seventeenth century, nature came to be considered a measurable, quantitative entity: "It was declared that there were no hierarchies in nature and the world no longer appeared as constructed for man or as the measure of man. All phenomena, like all component parts of a machine, were declared to have the same value."[26] Furthermore, under the influence of Cartesian doubt, people began to shift their focus from the outward appearance of objects to their concealed intrinsic structure. A major consequence of the seventeenth-century break with classical thought was a shift from interest in "what" to "how" – that is, from object to process. Process "was originally the fabrication process which disappears in the product, and it was based on the experience of *homo faber*, who knew that a production process necessarily precedes the actual existence of every object."[27] From this point on, process dominates the final product, while technology replaces *techne*. Unlike the latter, which signified the unity of work and meaning, technology takes nothing into account but the process of production.

In architectural discourse, the break with classical thought initiated a battle between ancients and moderns. Claude Perrault questioned the authority of classical treatises. For the first time, the idea that architecture was a totality – to which nothing could be added and from which nothing could be taken away – was challenged. Perrault proposed his simplified order based on a distinction between positive and arbitrary beauty. This distinction caused the logos of making to be dependent on the vicissitudes of various techniques of construction. Symbolic and analogical values of architecture thus gave way to a mode of understanding that was concerned mainly with the empirical aspects of building, that is, richness of material, delicacy of workmanship, and symmetry.[28] This analytical point of view undermined the ontological relationship between construction and type. Architectural elements, such as walls, columns, and beams, lost their poetic figuration; their meaning was abstracted. However, beauty, which was understood as an aspect of a given custom, found its theoretical justification in the Kantian sublime: the realm of "free" natural beauty and its inclusion in the formalist practice of the concept of autonomy.[29] This line of thought was pushed to its extreme by J. L. N. Durand, who conceived and classified architectural forms based on function and economy of use. By separating architectural types from the exigencies of their construction, Durand presented an abstract understanding of every element of architecture and placed each one in an empirical relationship with every other. His analytical view cleansed architecture from every mimetic effect in favor of the autonomy of architectural language.[30]

Theareafter, meaning was conceived of as inherent in form itself, which does not allude to anything outside, but to its syntactic role.

Long before this development took place, Galileo was exploring the relationship between column and beam.[31] Mapping the process of mechanization of design, Alexander Tzonis noticed that Galileo's observation and experimentation on the direct relationship between material and structural efficiency was a critical factor in the break between the modern mode of thinking and the archaic.[32] The echoes of Galileo's ideas were soon heard in architectural discourse. Laugier, in denouncing the "abuses" of Baroque architecture, postulated an architecture based on the structural and formal logic of the primitive hut. He argued for solidity in terms of "choice of material and efficient use."[33] For Laugier, "efficient use" was dependent on the "right" balance between force and load. The architectural discourse that he developed defined the significance of architectural elements in terms of their "structural utility."[34] He stated that "the vaults, the ceiling, the roof are the loads of a building and the walls its support. The planning architect should correctly estimate the force of loads so as to regulate with certainty the force of support."[35] Moreover, following a logic applied to the life process of natural objects, Laugier characterized style as a choice that relates to the "essence" of a building. All this foreshadowed what Foucault has characterized as a break with classical discourse or representation. According to him, the general area of knowledge in the eighteenth century was "no longer that of identities and differences, that of nonquantative orders, but an area made of organic structures, that is, of internal relations between elements whose totality performs a function."[36] The concept of organic structure was not totally a new theme. But its novelty, according to Foucault, lies in the fact that for the first time the idea of organic structure began to function as a method of characterization. Again, Durand translates Foucault's observation into architectural discourse: "If a building lends itself conveniently to the use for which it was destined, will it not naturally have a character and, more importantly, a character of its own?"[37]

In accordance with Foucault's concept of *epistem,* one might claim that in order for architecture to crumble under the weight of classical order, it had to do more than indulge in the problematic of positive and arbitrary beauties. Perrault's revolt from "classical doctrine" remained in the realm of ideas. The space was not yet constructed where Perrault could see arbitrary and positive beauties beyond the limits of the classical language of architecture. Certain conceptual discontinuities and scientific truths had to be identified in order to wean architecture from its classical poetics. To understand this paradox and its implications for the later development of the concept of construction, we must acknowledge the unique place of Etienne-Louis Boullée and his architecture. The geometry so dominant in his architecture was expressive, but not of the similarity between everyday life and the divine order, as in classical architecture. Nor did Boullée's geometry echo the usage of the Renaissance. Instead, Boullée said that the arrangement of a volume "should be such that we can absorb at a glance the multiplicity of the separate elements that constitute the whole." The result is an architectural object whose "character" can be effectively perceived by an observer.[38]

In Boullée's design for Newton's cenotaph, for example, the sphere was displaced from the realm of Platonic ideas and moved into the concrete domain of architectural discourse. This formal transformation merged with a discourse on the theme of death identical to that in J. L. David's painting *The Death of Marat,* which illustrates the self-sacrifice and patriotism of the body for the revolutionary soul.[39] The dialogue between body and soul attained its architectonic language in Boullée's work. In Newton's cenotaph, the sacred was removed from the body of death: its weight evaporated in the lightness of the geometry. Did Boullée know that in Newton's theories, as Italo Calvino has noted, "what most strikes the literary imagination is not the conditioning of everything and everyone by the inevitability of its own weight, but rather the balance of forces that enables heavenly bodies to float in space"?[40] Does not Boullée's floating geometry distinguish his architecture from classical architecture? Or does his discourse postulate that form, in its totality, is the subject of an autonomous architecture?

Certain aspects of not only Boullée's but Durand's architecture offer positive responses to these questions. In Newton's cenotaph, the relationship between inside and outside is not problematized within the discourse of anthropomorphism; rather, it is framed by the sublime. Anthony Vidler suggests that "the idea of classical architecture, which had never seen itself as a language, but only as a system of building conforming to laws of beauty, was now definitely superseded by an idea of architecture as expression." And he continues, "The role of architecture to construct was gradually reconstructed to that of to speak."[41]

This reconstruction retains another quality; that is, it problematizes the dichotomy between construction and ornament. Again one thinks of Alberti's suggestion that ornament elevates building into a phenomenon.[42] Boullée, in contrast, closes the gap between design and building and unfolds a space for the expressive aspect of his geometrical constructs.

The dissociation of eighteenth-century architecture from tradition should be seen as another step toward the secularization of architectural production. Yet this break presaged a state of anxiety that typified the nineteenth-century attitude as a concern for a proper style. Style, as defined by Laugier, was understood to be an aspect of the "destination" of a building. However, in the discourse of early modernism, technology transcended all cultural values; it signified a means for securing rational activity. Ironically, in the course of its development, technology was defined not only as the process of making, but more important, as the "destination" of the building itself, changing the metaphorical province of the subject.

TECTONIC: THE IN-BETWEEN OF CONSTRUCTION
AND SIGNIFICATION

The concept of the tectonic has become critical for contemporary theories of architecture. In order to map the vicissitudes of the tectonic, we need to discuss the esteem of nineteenth-century architects in incorporating a steel frame into masonry construction. Although the poetics of *techne* had already been pushed into the background by Laugier, Viollet-le-Duc could still frame his reading of the duality between lineaments and matter in Gothic architecture. Herbert Damisch presents a structuralist reading of Viollet-le-Duc's *Dictionary*.[43] He argues that Viollet-le-Duc's analysis of the different components of architecture and their morphological development suggests a structuralist interpretation of the relationship between the architectural whole and its parts. Going beyond the prevailing academic views of his time, Viollet-le-Duc visualized the duality of form and construction as similar to the relationship between a whole and its part. Accordingly, rather than the reality of the stones and mortar in Gothic architecture, he saw a model, in the structuralist sense of the word. "The visible framework, the trac-

ery of ribbing and salient features which are thrown over the
masonry like a net," Damisch notes, "immediately suggests
to the observer a structuralist scheme which certainly does
not correspond to a theory of construction."[44] Damisch concludes that, for Viollet-le-Duc, the truth of architecture rests
not in the empirical reality of its material, nor in its compositional form, but somewhere between form and substance,
or between architecture and construction.

Karl Botticher points out the dialectics at work in the history of architecture as well. In contrast to the followers of
Greek and Gothic architecture, Botticher advocated a third
style that would "reject neither of the two preceding ones but
will base itself on the achievements of both in order to occupy a third stage in the development, a higher stage than
either."[45] The same dialectical approach was suggested in
Viollet-le-Duc's reading of Gothic architecture, where not
only the "Greek genius for structural formulations and the
Roman gift for programmatic planning" were at work; the
"principal lines of construction," as he would like to say, also
evolved out of a synthesis of the ribs, emulating vertical support, and the walls, which provide nothing but enclosure.[46]
Viollet-le-Duc found in the Gothic a proper model for
nineteenth-century architecture. By means of it he could rethink traditional masonry construction in conjunction with
the structural possibilities offered by a steel frame.

His model broke new ground for nineteenth-century architecture, whose language was either limited to the Beaux
Arts revision of Vitruvian discourse or else took for granted
the factuality of the glass and steel frame, as did John Paxton
in the Crystal Palace. Viollet-le-Duc's interest in bringing together traditional masonry construction and steel frame
structure is important if one recalls Semper's thought on the
relationship between earthwork and framework. Also important for a discussion of the tectonic is the idea of the joint,
which is at work in any architectonic articulation of masonry
and frame systems, namely, "the insertion of a prefabricated
fireproof iron assembly into a masonry shell which had been
tectonically prepared to receive it," as Kenneth Frampton
observes.[47] In this "preparation" the joint is made to function as an ornament, which, contrary to Ruskin, is not
"fixed on"[48] but becomes an indispensable part of the tectonic form. Viollet-le-Duc seems to have been aware of this
aspect of his theory; he stated clearly that ornament should be
consistent with the material employed and in harmony with
the structure and the first conception of the program.[49]

These words suggest the closing of the gap between architecture and building, a subject interesting enough to occupy the first pages of Ruskin's *Seven Lamps of Architecture*. Ruskin reminds us, "It is very necessary, at the outset of all inquiry, to distinguish carefully between Architecture and Building," and he continues, "Let us therefore, at once, confine the name architecture to the art that, taking up and admitting, as conditions of its working, the necessities and common uses of the building, impresses on its form certain characters venerable or beautiful, but otherwise unnecessary."[50] Viollet-le-Duc avoids the idea that ornament is a supplement by asserting that ornament occupies its well-defined position when "the structure of the architectural features constitutes the ornamentation." Such an ontological understanding of the relationship between the logic of construction and ornamentation is at work in Viollet-le-Duc's reading of the Venetian ducal palace; looking at the facade, Viollet-le-Duc asks: "Do we not see that the lower portico is vaulted, and that the upper one supports a timber floor – the floor of the apartments above – and that the ceilings of these apartments are of wood? No projecting buttresses or pilasters for the upper story, which is nothing other than a box perforated with great windows."[51] I will come back to the idea of the joint and its import for the tectonic shortly. At this point, however, it should be stressed that this discussion does not place Semper in line with Viollet-le-Duc. Rather, he departs not only from the nineteenth-century problematic, but from the very structuralist thinking of Viollet-le-Duc. Although Viollet-le-Duc never discussed the question of the tectonic in the terms articulated here, certain homologies are to be found between Viollet-le-Duc's and other major architectural theories of the nineteenth century. Even Viollet-le-Duc's opinion that "the best architecture is that whose ornamentation cannot be divorced from the structure" could be associated with Ruskin's concern for moral issues in architectural production. Pugin's argument that a valid detail is one that is structurally significant also comes to mind in this connection.[52] To formulate a theory of architecture that could respond not only to new building types and technologies, but also to the very idea of the loss of history, nineteenth-century architects found that they needed to push the symbolic element of architecture into the shadows; in fact, most of the nineteenth-century yearning for style was nothing but an expression of that thematic shift of interest. Viollet-le-Duc's discourse is important because it implies the idea of the tec-

tonic, as well as his belief that architecture is not an imitative
art. By saying that style is not a garment to cover a building – a statement that, at times, might be misused because of
its sensational and visual content – Viollet-le-Duc came close
to Semper, who related the psychology of an architect to that
of a musician.[53] Yet the spatiality of Semper's discourse, the
way he mapped the limits of architecture among different
production activities – a position that shifts architecture
from its classical foundation – put him in line with current
poststructuralist thinking.

Now, why should one speak of Semper's tectonic at the
historical moment that is marked by the death of subject
and simulation?[54] Frampton has already discussed the significance of the tectonic for an alternative theory of architecture.[55] My intention, however, is to read Semper in light of
Walter Benjamin's disbelief in the possibility of a genuine experience of tradition. This is not an arbitrary juxtaposition. It
is my contention that, to some extent, Semper's thought alludes to what Benjamin would later call the dissolution of the
aura in the context of the mechanization of the process of
production.[56]

In his essay "The Storyteller," Benjamin reminds us of the
peculiar way in which the form of a novel orders historical
events in order to reflect the modern concept of experience.[57]
For Benjamin, storytelling takes place in a web where the exchange of experience between the individual and the group is
not yet contaminated by information. Benjamin believes that
this interconnection between the storyteller and the listeners
is taken from circumstance: "Never has experience been con-
tradicted more thoroughly than strategic experience by tac-
tical warfare, economic experience by inflation . . . , and
bodily experience by mechanical warfare."[58] For Benjamin,
the shocking and violent experiences that impinge upon everyday life in the Metropolis have transformed the entire
structure of human experience. Accordingly, the mechanization of production has made it impossible to transfer tradition, including the craft of architecture, from hand to hand
and by word of mouth. In contrast, the demise of the classical
language of architecture attests to a state of fragmentation in
which tradition can be remembered only in isolated experiences. It is this last point, the devaluation of tradition and the
resulting disintegration of remembrance, by which I intend
to relate Semper's thought to poststructuralist discourse.

In *Science, Industry, and Art,* Semper suggested that architecture had lost its classical totality, so that it was almost im-

possible to think of a coherent body of knowledge developed around a center. As he traced the evolution of the "high" arts from their many conflicting and alien motives, he suggested that "architecture must step down from its throne and go into the market-place, there to teach and to learn."[59] Semper thus unfolds a nihilistic discourse somewhat similar to neo-avant-gardism. Aware of the anomalies of capitalism, Semper was forced to consider the process of cultural secularization to be a critical point of departure for his theory. As opposed to his contemporaries, who nostalgically dreamed of the survival of craftsmanship and the Gothic guilds, Semper suggested that "this process of disintegrating existing art types must be completed by industry, by speculation, and by applied science before something good and new can result."[60]

But Semper's hermeneutical understanding of the "new" sets him apart from the general modernist dislike of history. In fact, I would suggest that the concept of the new in Semper is an essential part of the spatiality of his thought. As he witnessed the disappearance of traditional forms of art, Semper mapped a theory that integrated ur-forms with new techniques and materials.[61] His theoretical problem was to discover the means of transcending the limits of historicism. In *The Four Elements of Architecture,* one is lured by a sense of deconstruction at work when Semper proposes that architecture has evolved out of the experience of four divided industries. This bases architectural knowledge in the two primordial forms of dwelling: the earthwork, or the act of marking the site to receive a building (thereby responding to the forces of gravity and its architectonic realization in the act of framing) and the framework, a detailed procedure in which the contradiction between heaviness and lightness, enclosure and exposure are articulated artistically. Semper thus anticipates the predicament of logocentrism and opens a "spatiality" through which architecture could be loosed from the ground of historicism to become subject to the dynamics of cultural secularization. That opening, interestingly enough, resonates with the spatial transparencies that are perceptible in the screen of mass-media technology.

Ceramics, carpentry, masonry, and weaving were the four industrial arts that correspond to the four elements of architecture (Figure 2). The hearth, or the center, derives its forms and ideas from ceramics and metalwork. The roof, mound (terrace), and enclosure were related to the skills developed in carpentry, masonry, and weaving, respectively. Of these elements, the hearth and the roof were essential parts of the

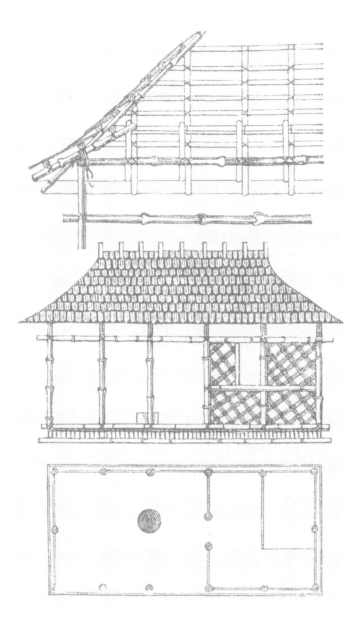

Figure 2. The hut on display at the Great Exhibition, London, 1851. From Gottfried Semper, *Der Stil* (1860). The Resource Collection of the Getty Center for the History of Art and the Humanities, Santa Monica, California.

earliest forms of dwelling. Here, Semper's main objective was to support his argument for the polychromatic character of Greek architecture. He emphasized the importance of enclosure, and its connection with carpeting, for spatial definition and division. He claimed that wickerwork "was the *essence of the wall*," and in a footnote continued: "The German word *Wand* [wall], *paries*, acknowledges its origin. The terms *Wand* and *Gewand* [dress] derive from a single root. They indicate the woven material that formed the wall."[62] For Semper the glazed and painted walls of ancient architecture reflected the texture of the carpet hanging from the masonry wall. It is interesting that Semper's discussion of the relationship between the hanging carpet and the protective wall is oriented from the inside: "Hanging carpets remained the true walls, the visible boundaries of space. The often solid walls *behind* them were necessary for reasons that had nothing to do with the creation of space; they were needed for security, for supporting a load, for their permanence, and so on."[63]

The word "behind" raises two points. In reading Semper, one cannot avoid the importance of the inside–outside or, as he would phrase it later, the *Kernform* (core-form) and *Kunstform* (art-form). For him the moral aspect of architecture was the core-form, the hearth; in fact, the whole of Western architecture exhibits only different tectonic forms of the Asiatic enclosed court architecture: "The pyramids were nothing more than colossal substructures for the object actually intended – a tomb or a temple." Semper offers the same reading for the Greek temples, as well as for the Gothic cathedrals, which are vaulted basilicas: "a court with its central open space interiorized by placing a high roof over it."[64] This esteem for the hearth, however, places Semper's discourse beyond the perspectival vision of the Renaissance, which conceives of architecture either as a form in itself or an aesthetic object analogous to the fine arts.

However, Semper's departure from humanistic discourse was not total. Mapping the prospects of the idea of dressing (*Bekleidung*), Semper reserves some room for the painter. To preserve the original meaning of the wall, Semper suggests that one should not avoid dressing both the interior and the exterior of the wall with paint. One thinks of Loos's text *Das Prinzip der Bekleidung* or Mark Wigley's recent association of Le Corbusier's white architecture with Semper's dressing.[65] While Loos remained faithful to Semper's stress on the importance of the hearth, the interior, and its relationship with the exterior, Wigely seems to be motivated by Semper's idea that "antique polychromy lost its historical basis once the wall's material and construction recovered their high artistic value with the Romans. No longer were material and construction subordinate features hidden behind a partition wall (*Scheerwand*), merely serving; they began to create form, or at least to influence it."[66] It is true that the idea of dressing denies the material basis of architecture, but as Semper's interpretation of the Greek column suggests, the final form is a symbolic articulation and masking of "the column's static role, while also denying its material basis."[67] If this is a plausible statement for a distinction between atectonic and tectonic form, then it is hard to see how Le Corbusier's white architecture evolves out of a symbolic relationship between the core-form and the art-form.

Wolfgang Herrmann suggests that the tectonic was an important theme in Semper's thought from the time he read Botticher, who, alone among the nineteenth-century advocates of a new style, argued for a synthesis of the principles of Greco-Gothic architecture. According to him, this new style could not arise from stone or other conventional materials, mainly because their structural and spatial potentialities were already exhausted.[68] Like Viollet-le-Duc, Botticher was interested in iron and its structural principles, searching for the formation of a new system of covering space. The means of covering a space was the essence of Botticher's discourse on the core-form and the art-form. With all styles, he argued, "the covering is the factor that determines the placing and configuration of the structural supports, as well as the arrangement and articulation of the walls by which space is enclosed, and finally the art-forms of all those parts are related to it."[69] How to give a proper form or, to put it in Botticher's words, "a kind of explanatory layer" to a system of enclosing spaces is the point of departure for a tectonic form. In this context, the art-form neither represents the subjective intentions of the architect nor expresses the physicality of a structural system. Rather, the intention of the art-form is to "symbolize the concept of structure and space that in its purely structural state cannot be perceived."[70] Drawing from Botticher's reflections on the art-form and the core-form, Semper defined the tectonic as a cosmic art analogous to music and dance. "Tectonics deals with the product of human artistic skills, not with its utilitarian aspect but solely with that part that reveals a conscious attempt by the artisan to express cosmic laws and cosmic order when molding the material."[71] In this sense, the art-form does not express itself as an aesthetic form independent of the core-form. Rather, as he observes about Hellenic art, Semper reveals the art-form as it relates to the core-form: in "a *structural-symbolic* rather than in a *structural-technical* sense."[72]

The structural-symbolic relationship discussed by both Botticher and Semper suggests the import of Semper's theory of dressing and its intimate connection to architecture. It also clarifies the structural function of the wall (or any other load-bearing system) and its "revealed poetics" – a term coined by Frampton – in the final work. This does not limit itself "to a type of tendentious decorative adornment of surfaces with sculpture and painting, but essentially conditions the art-form in general." In Greek architecture, Semper writes, "both the *art-form and decoration are so intimately bound together by the influence of the principle of surface dressing that an isolated look at either is impossible.*"[73] This is far beyond Viollet-le-Duc's positivistic understanding of construction and the humanistic tradition of interpreting ornament as an addition. For Viollet-le-Duc, form is the realization of construction and material; however, for Semper, the tectonic evolves out of the metamorphosis of material and the skills that were already at work in both costume and festive structures (Figure 3). In this metamorphosis, or, to use Semper's term, *Stoffwelchsel,* the joint – originally derived from the knot in textiles – plays a critical role (Figure 4). The joint is, in fact, an inseparable part of a tectonic form: it brings our attention to the surface, not to express the nature of materials or the physicality of the construction, but to unfold the intrinsic essence of the enclosure and the characteristic of the space enclosed. One can compare the importance of the joint for tectonic form with the symbolic significance and the metaphysical implications of the cross in Renaissance architecture. It should be stressed that our very understanding of this metaphysics is implied in the concept of the joint, which may be said to bring together the matter and the body. The congruity between construction and construing is essential for the production of architecture. According to Marco Frascari, through detail one can see "the process of signification; that is, the attaching of meanings to man-produced objects. The details are then the *locii* where knowledge is of an order in which the mind finds its own working, that is, *logos.*"[74]

Besides the joint, there are two other aspects to the ideas just considered that are important for an understanding of the discussion of montage that follows. First, there is the generic structure of Semper's thought, which sees architectural production in relation to techniques developed in other industries. "How to change old forms, consecrated by necessity and tradition, according to our new means of fabrication" becomes Semper's motto on the tectonic. Semper propounds an associative understanding of architecture, in which a building is a fragment of a larger reality: it becomes the construction of the conditions of life. In other words, the intercommunication between various industries constitutes a chain of constructive syntaxes that are the material condition of what Heinrich Hubsch calls the "technostatic experience."[75]

Second, Botticher stresses the significance of structural-spatial combinations for art-forms. Thus, both the material and technical results of other constructive works, as well as their implications for our spatial experience, constitute the obscurity of meaning and the complexity of architecture. Accordingly, one can argue that Semper's four elements of architecture are not formal categories. These elements of dwelling may represent some moments of life, as they are experienced through ceramics, joinery, masonry, and textiles.

Aegyptisches Kapitäl.

Figure 3. Egyptian capital with lotus flower inserts and Persian capital with volutes imitating Assyrian hollow-body construction. From Gottfried Semper, *Der Stil* (1860). The Resource Collection of the Getty Center for the History of Art and the Humanities, Santa Monica, California.

Figure 4. Knots. From Gottfried Semper, *Der Stil* (1860). The Resource Collection of the Getty Center for the History of Art and the Humanities, Santa Monica, California.

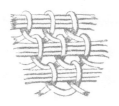

Yet our experience of these four arts is not limited to their material and technical dimensions. Each technostatic experience also contains a particular "spatial practice": the dialectical relationship between perceived, conceived, and lived spaces.[76] It was therefore not merely the economic and material dimensions of iron that informed the nineteenth-century debate on style, but its structural-spatial potentialities as well. To rethink the tectonic, one should first map the vicissitudes of the technostatic experience.

The idea of montage parallels the art of construction; but montage also has to do with the secularization of cultural production. Developed out of cinematography and shared by different industries, the making of a montage is a process that permeates a structural-spatial experience far beyond that of nineteenth-century architects.

Montage also empties the natural content of an organic understanding of the concept of construction, or to put it in Benjamin's words, the aura of *techne* and the tectonic. To this end it is important to mention the similarities between montage and sewing; both modes of making bring together fragmented pieces, leaving the seam for ornamental purposes. This anology is interesting when one also notices the material differences between cotton felt and woven fabric within the textile industry. The latter follows the most conspicuous characteristics of a Cartesian vision of making: hierarchy, which is a sense of directionality from the lowest to the highest level, and symmetry. The former, however, made of diverse fabrics and without following any preconceived plan, can be spread in different directions and forms. Yet the spatial differences between felt and fabric discussed by Gilles Deleuze and Félix Guattari convincingly suggest the import of montage and its spatial constructs for the demythification of the classical discourse on construction.[77] For example, montage dispenses with the analogies that classicism draws between the human body and architecture, or the concept of the hearth as discussed by Semper, and restores the art of construction according to its contemporary perceptual and technical experience.

The historical progression of secularization should also figure in the discussion. It undermines filiative relations (and even the very concept of dwelling, which connects one to a place) in favor of affiliative or transpersonal relationships. We can therefore trace the transformation of relationships from organic to cultural,[78] and the same metamorphosis relates montage to the tectonic. Montage disconnects the relation of

the whole to the part that is essential to the classical discourse
on construction. Its concept of the whole is neither representational nor the logical result of a hierarchical composition of
its parts, whether it is discussed in terms of the Vitruvian
triad or the principle of three-part composition shared by
some modern architects. Instead, the whole arises out of the
juxtaposition of fragments and by the act of montage itself,
and therein lies the dialectic between intention and construction, or as Semper would say, in the structural-symbolic. In
this understanding of the whole, the coherent totality of architectural form is weakened, and montage plays a significant
role in generating a tectonic form.

Montage reveals its tectonic form in the "dis-joint"
(seam?), a weak form that distances sign from signifier. Traditionally, the function of the joint was to cover the anomalies of construction and to create the illusion of an aesthetic
unity. The "dis-joint," in contrast, integrates material and
detailing in such a way that the final form, somewhat like a
well-crafted movie, does not completely hide the fragmented
process of its production.

In this "distanciation,"[79] which is not factual and spatial,
architecture attains semantic autonomy by problematizing
the event of its inception, that is, the humanist myth and the
subjective expressions of the architect. By separating architecture from these two poles, construction (perhaps "fabrication" would be a better term) emerges as the sole semantic
dimension of architecture. Fabrication, then, should be understood dialectically. Ontologically, then, we understand
architecture as a fabric, the etymology of which signifies
both the style or plan of construction and a woven material.
Yet after the loss of the aura and the intensification of the experience of fragmentation, the art-form should stress the fact
that the perceived spatial envelope is, literally, a fabrication: it
is a falsehood. The emphasis on the nihilistic connotation of
fabrication substantiates the contention that the separation of
sign and signifier is historical. The modern age opens an epoch in which "appearance and essence together cease to exist," and "at the level of consciousness, the only possible
hermeneutic is that of suspicion."[80] The same is true for the
idea of fabrication: whereas the nineteenth century conceived
construction as bounded by the ethical values of craftsmanship, fabrication presents itself as natural, similar to the way
in which a commodity's "mystical" character depends on the
fact that its value is "disconnected from its specific use value
and the concrete labor that produced it."[81] Moreover, the dif-

ferences Benjamin draws between the novel and storytelling, and the distinctions Ricoeur makes between speaking and writing, attest to the fact that in the process of transformation from an organic state of thinking and making into a mechanized one, technique has prevailed. This is not a green light for an arbitrary exploitation of the sign; rather, it requires that we rethink the tectonic by recollecting the thematics that bind sign and signifier. Here, recollection is not intended to correct what went wrong in such a time and place or to construct a nostalgic remembrance of some forgotten past. Recollection is a countermemory that "distorts," to use Gianni Vattimo's word,[82] any hegemonic characterization of the relationship between sign and signifier.

This emphasis on the manufactured signifier and its mute existence makes apparent the hidden factors determining the work and the conditions under which it is perceived. It will become evident that the loss of the center and the importance given to fabrication elevate the process of secularization in architectural production. Montage is a technique that drains the metaphysics of the tectonic and unfolds a new way of being in the world. As Ricoeur suggests, this is a dialectical process by which the "otherness" of an autonomous cultural product anchors itself within a given cultural experience, and this appropriation is the poetic task of montage.

CHAPTER 2

ARCHITECTURE AND THE QUESTION OF TECHNOLOGY

Two Positions and the "Other"

In the classical treatises on architecture, there is no understanding of technology as it is known today. The absence of
the modern concept of technology as a theme in classical discourse on architecture was due to the ontological bond between art and science as represented by the word *techne*. In
Vitruvian and Palladian discourses on architecture, *techne*
signifies the logos of making: a concept of fabrication in
which technique is congenial with the image of the final object itself.

Toward the end of the seventeenth century, *techne* in its
classical sense was replaced by "technique," or the manner in
which an artist or artisan uses the technical elements of an art
or a craft. With the advent of mechanization in the late eighteenth century, the ontological relationship between art and
science disappeared. In its later usage, "technique" provided
solutions for problems without necessarily evincing any particular concern with the object of the problem or its historical
values. Parallel to these developments is the appearance in the
mid-nineteenth century of an architectural discourse in which
positive rationality takes over the logos of making.

Writing during the Gothic revival, William Morris and
Eugène-Emmanuel Viollet-le-Duc promoted a type of architectural discourse that, in its specificity, broke away from the
Romantic movement and from the language of classical architecture. Viollet-le-Duc, in "Architecture in the Nineteenth Century – Importance of Method,"[1] and Morris, in
"The Revival of Architecture,"[2] introduced two interrelated
themes into architectural discourse: the first theme was historicism, which implied that the sociocultural values of a
product are historically determined. In his argument with
Gothic revivalists, Viollet-le-Duc asked, "Is the nineteenth
century destined to close without possessing an architecture

of its own?"[3] Criticizing the same trend of thought, Morris proposed that the art of any epoch must of necessity be the expression of its social life. The concept of a temporal relationship between architecture and its epoch was unfolding.

The second theme was progress – that is, a search for social improvement through technological improvements. It is not necessary here to dwell on Viollet-le-Duc's esteem for the use of new materials in architecture. We should rather give attention to the dichotomy between technology and the moral values of tradition in Morris's thought. Morris was critical of the industrial developments of his time because of their impact on moral values. Nevertheless, his vision of the "pleasure of work" proposes an industrial technology integrated with the ethics and morality of the guild system.[4]

These issues were epitomized in the ideas of the Werkbund and the Bauhaus schools, the development of which has been attributed to the socioeconomic condition of Germany. They also appeared in the school of critical thought primarily expressed in the periodical *Das Andere* (The Other).[5] One of the contributors, Adolf Loos, declared war on old customs and the artistic values of Secessionism.[6] Although Loos was critical of the Werkbund and the Bauhaus, he nevertheless advised his native craftspeople to follow the path of their Anglo-Saxon fellows. For all intents and purposes, however, it was Peter Behrens who for the first time positively advocated the idea of progress and the improvement of artifacts via architects' collaboration with industry.

Was it not through Behrens's office that Walter Gropius conceived the idea of promoting an alignment of architecture with the production line, as was the case with Behrens's designed artifacts? And again, was it not from the same environment that the French celebrity suggested that architecture should be purified of its historical language, so that abstraction could become the vehicle of the realization of a "new objectivity"? These two questions are the subject matter of the following pages, in which they will be examined in the context of the architectural discourses of Gropius and Le Corbusier.

"PROCESS": THE IMPERATIVE OF TECHNOLOGY

The architectural thought that characterized the early twentieth century had a heterogeneous character. The Bauhaus school, in its initial phase, represented the viewpoints of architects who generally favored a change in the cultural values and artifacts of daily life. Later, by laying particular stress on a closer relationship with industry, the school strayed from its initial path. The architect of the transformation was Gropius. Under his leadership and afterward, the Bauhaus became first an indirect and later a direct body part of German industrial bourgeois planning.

A brief look at the signet used in different periods of the school helps us to follow the direction that Gropius determined. The signet used up to 1921 signifies an ontological understanding of human beings and shelter (Figure 5). The hipped roof held up by a human figure posits a vernacular origin for architecture, one much in accord with the concept of Marc-Antoine Laugier's hut. The signet used after 1921 illustrates the domination of technology over humanity (Figure 6). The human face on the signet does not possess any figurative element; it is one-dimensional and abstract. Vertical and horizontal lines are the main compositional elements, which are framed in a circle. Ironically, since then, the circle has symbolized the industrial myth. Indeed, the later signet represents the two major aspects of the Modern movement — that is, abstraction and technology.

In his discourse, Gropius dwells on the debris of Morris's view of craftsmanship. The differences between these two poles of architectural thought, which for Nikolaus Pevsner define a "historical unit,"[7] are, indeed, historical. In Germany, the critical content, "joy of labor," was molded by positivism. For Gropius, the machine and collaboration with industrialists was a necessity, while for Morris the whole idea was problematic.

Figure 5. Signet of the Stattliche Bauhaus, from 1919 to 1921. From Hans M. Wingler, *The Bauhaus: Weimar, Dessau, Berlin and Chicago* (Cambridge, Mass.: MIT Press, 1969).

Figure 6. Signet of the Stattliche Bauhaus, after a design by Oskar Schlemmer, 1922. From Hans M. Wingler, *The Bauhaus: Weimar, Dessau, Berlin and Chicago* (Cambridge, Mass.: MIT, Press, 1969).

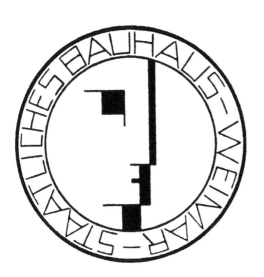

Gropius's positivistic understanding of architecture is prevalent in one of his earliest texts, entitled "Gropius at Twenty-Six," which was first published in 1910.[8] The article was written as a guideline for a company to produce prefabricated houses; nevertheless, the article expresses the "party line" of the future school. It promotes the idea of the "happy union" of art and technique. Historically, the idea was not new: Matei Calinescu has observed that, toward the end of his life, Saint-Simon "regarded artists, along with scientists, and industrialists as naturally destined to be part of the trinitarian ruling elite in the ideal state."[9] Saint Simon's idea was not realized during his lifetime, but Gropius's hope, partly in practice at the Werkbund school, became the primary motive of the Bauhaus institution. The problematic aspect of Gropius's thought was his sociological understanding of architecture.

In *Scope of Total Architecture,* Gropius presented an architectural discourse that was laden with themes and concepts from sociology. The architect is characterized as a "true planner" who can recognize the correct position of each participant in planning. According to Gropius, the aim was to snatch "the creative artist from his other-worldliness" and deposit him into "the workaday world of realities." In addition, education became a tool to "broaden and humanize the rigid . . . material mind of the businessmen." All this was aimed at preparing the condition for a "new generation of architects in close contact with modern means of production."[10] On another occasion, Gropius stated that the idea was to "form a new guild of craftsmen without the class distinctions which raised an arrogant barrier between craftsman and artists."[11]

In fact, a desire for medieval-like lodges by Gropius was not a romantic quest. Nor is it understandable in the context of a dichotomy between nature and culture. One might discern Morris's ideas in Rousseau's discourse, which distinguishes nature from its "other" – technology and artifact. But Gropius's interest in crafts, and craftpersons' participation in the "future guild," is totally different. Morris, in his struggle against the alienation of industrial work, was seduced by the myth of handwork and its beauty. Gropius, in contrast, misrepresents the differences between craft and industrial technology and thus dismisses the whole issue of secularization.

A formative concept in German discourse on crafts and the machine resides in the German word *Handwerk,* literally meaning "hand labor." More elaboration of this word comes from Theodore Adorno, who states that *Handwerk* refers "to modes of production proper to a rudimentary economy that have been lost in the triumph of technology and degraded by their picturesque disinterment by representatives of the Modern Style."[12] Adorno's interpretation should be understood in relation to the historical rupture that separates the craftspersons' work from later technical progress. Yet Marcel Franciscono's remark on this word is more in line with the Bauhaus thought. On this issue, Franciscono states: "Handwerk does not have, and had even less in the time of the Bauhaus, the restricted meaning that 'handicraft' has in English. It denotes the manual disciplines in general . . . it also takes into consideration division of labor, as handicraft does not."[13] This understanding of *Handwerk* is shared by Gropius when he differentiates industry from craftsmanship as "far less to the different nature of the tools employed in each, than to subdivision of labor in one and undivided control by a single workman in the latter." Moreover, "handicraft and industry may be regarded as opposite poles that are gradually approaching each other."[14]

It goes without saying that when mechanized modes of production appeared, the two "poles" were wrenched apart. In the mechanization of production, the artifact was detached from its domain of tradition. For Walter Benjamin, this change – the "destruction of aura" – has profound consequences for the "authenticity" of artifact.[15] Industrial production necessitated not only different tools, but also a new perception of nature and object. The mind's eye of the craftsperson and the anthropocentric nature of craftsmanship could not function in a process that recognizes the rationale of mechanization as its prime principle. In looking back to craftsmanship, Gropius confines his canon to the process of making without grasping Benjamin's concept of aura and its historical and cultural significance.

The implication of Gropius's views on art and technology is a design concept in which the process of making undermines the metaphorical and symbolic aspects. The reader of Gropius will not find it difficult to discern an empirical understanding of architecture. One can cite Gropius's discussion of the Georgian window as an example of his empiricism: "The confining, cage-like Georgian windows, which in their time were necessary due to limitations in manufacturing of glass, have been supplanted by large window openings and undivided glass panes."[16] Of course, no one can argue against the limitations of certain historical production techniques, but it is a grave simplification to attribute a one-to-one correspondence between technological developments and architectonic transformation. We will see how this view would reduce architecture to the status of a mere industrial utensil.

SPIRIT OF TIME AND THE NEW OBJECTIVITY

Heinrich Wolfflin has characterized the years around 1800 as the renewal of a linear mode of vision, which "comes to serve a new objectivity."[17] The architectonic implications of Wolfflin's discourse might be pursued in the tenth lecture of Viollet-le-Duc's *Entretiens*. There symmetry as the general law of architecture is questioned, and a formal composition based on harmony and equilibrium is proposed.[18] Viollet-le-Duc's dislike of classical norms of composition and his attempt to rearticulate architecture by means of industrial techniques and materials could be associated with certain aspects of a general artistic tendency in the late nineteenth century whose rejection of academia opened up a realistic view of art and literature.[19] Later in 1923, Gropius spoke for an architecture that is emptied of any semantic or formal traces of Wolfflin's discourse. Gropius's concern was neither historicism nor "naturalism" – two important themes for realist art and literature – but rather the "new objectivity" outlined as follows:

A new aesthetic of horizontal is beginning to develop which endeavors to counteract the effect of gravity. At the same time the symmetrical relationship of parts of the building and their orientation towards a central axis is being replaced by a new conception of equilibrium which transmutes this dead symmetry of similar parts into an asymmetrical but rhythmical balance.[20]

A new formal understanding of the architectural object emerged. This theme was optimized in thoughts of certain architectural circles in Russia and Germany. Without underestimating the significance of national boundaries, it is my contention that particular revelations of this objective mode of expression crystallized the homogeneous nature of the Modern movement. Nevertheless, one can discern three schools of thought in the early Modern movement.

The Bauhaus's view of the new objectivity is rooted in the German word *Sachlichkeit*. In various disciplines the word

is interpreted and applied differently. In painting, G. F. Hartlaub coined it in a letter appealing to painters who might like
to participate in an exhibition in Mannheim in 1923.[21] The
exhibition aimed to present those works that were faithful to
positive, palpable reality (*Sachlichkeit*). Sharing this reverence
for formal objectivity, in architecture *Sachlichkeit* does have
other connotations. One of its implications, cited by Fritz
Schmalenbach, is "anti-formalism."[22] Hartlaub, as noted,
defined *Sachlichkeit* in terms of a sober, minimally orna-
mented design in conformity with the purpose of its object.
Central to his concept was the architectonic implications of
bürgerlich (related to the English word "burgher"), implying
a humble, practical, and straightforward approach to a problem. This latter understanding of the word was popularized
by Hermann Muthesius in the Werkbund disputes.[23] Muthesius is a controversial figure for both his vagueness on
norm/type and for his administrative and political mission: to
shape the cultural space of an industrialized Germany. This
picture of Muthesius prompts one to suggest that he was the
key in a functionalist reading of *Neue Sachlichkeit*.[24] Among
disciples of the Werkbund, *Sachlichkeit* designated a design
concept in which the formal quality of architecture is demar-
cated from its technical and material aspects. In that context,
Behrens's view of design would have had merit: he put "order and absolute *Gestaltung* above matters ostensibly promoted by material and structure."[25] Behrens's architecture
presents a classical sobriety and clarity that stems from his
pessimistic interpretation of *Sachlichkiet*.

Since it was congenial to the Bauhaus emphasis on technology, an empirical view of *Sachlichkiet* was promoted. The
fundamental issue was the idea that artifacts, including architecture, must be transformed and enhanced in conformity
with technological development. "As history shows,"
Gropius maintains, "the conception of beauty has changed
along with progress in thought and technique."[26] From this
point of view, the machine by its perfect utility, its economy
of parts, its simplicity, and its beauty becomes the ideal
model for artistic creativity.

In his opposition to academic formalism, Gropius arrived
at a new understanding of the artifact. For him, a thing was
determined by its "nature," which "must answer its purpose in every way, that is, to fulfill its function in a practical
sense, and must thus be serviceable, reliable and cheap."[27]
Gropius observed that such requirements were fulfilled in

technology and engineering. Industry and machinery, therefore, became stimuli for architects. This idea finds its ultimate expression in his declaration "Art and technology, a new unity."

In Gropius's discourse, architecture, which throughout its classical period had responded to nature and human needs by means of allegory and morphology, turns its back on history and enters into a dialogue with the machine. From the world of technology and engineering, new themes and concepts permeated architectural discourse. In its dialogue with the machine, architecture was reduced to the status of a daily utensil, and its design mirrored the course of a production line. As a result, as with artifacts of industry, architecture lost its figurative elements and became a sober, palpable functional object.

Le Corbusier's view of the new objectivity was more original. *Towards a New Architecture* appealed for an architecture that was compositionally disciplined and, at the same time, objective. To achieve this goal, Le Corbusier set for himself the task of neutralizing the symbolic load of the elements of architecture.

Le Corbusier had the chance to see the Werkbund experiment during his short tenure with Behrens. Impressed by Behrens's ability to reconcile historical forms with new materials and needs, Le Corbusier formulated an architectural language that was not confined by the datum of industry, utility, and classical figures. In this regard, the idea behind Dom-i-no functioned as the "deep structure" of Le Corbusier's architectural language.

Designed in 1914, Dom-i-no is a frame system of reinforced concrete construction that discloses the two major aspects of Le Corbusier's architecture: first, its break with the classical language of architecture, and second, its self-referential capacity as an aesthetic object. This self-referential aspect of Dom-i-no has been analyzed in some depth by Peter Eisenman. Only its implications for "objectivity" need to be considered here.[28] To promote the spirit of mass consumption, Le Corbusier set out to redefine the architectural object. For him, "object-type" was the spirit of the time that was purified from historical dust and debris.[29] According to Stanislaus von Moos, this concept of objectivity was first presented by Charles Blanc, some of whose work Le Corbusier had read.[30] Blanc perceived that the coming generation would grasp the spirit of a thing and discard whatever was not exceptional and conspicuous. For architecture, this would mean discharging figurative representation through-out the elements of wall, beam, column, and roof.

In questioning the validity and undermining much of the figural character of the classical language of architecture, Le Corbusier was not unprecedented. In the late eighteenth and early nineteenth centuries, through classification and decomposition, J. L. N. Durand proposed various architectural configurations based on function and economy of use. Evidently his architecture did not have any relationship to what Vitruvian architecture defined as the "art of building." The maintenance of integrity between the representation and the building of architectural figures is the major characteristic of Vitruvian architecture. By separating architectural figures from the total image of architecture, Durand conceived the objectivity of every element of architecture in an empirical relationship with every other one. Thus, an early concept of architecture conceived according to a positivistic canon was realized by Durand. But Le Corbusier went beyond Durand. Le Corbusier discarded not only the classical forms, but their representational economy. To this end, the machine became a new metaphor. Such mechanical metaphors are fundamental to the modernist discourse on art. Matei Calinescu has traced the aesthetic relationship between art and machine back to Baudelaire. According to this nineteenth-century French literary figure, "A painting is a machine whose systems are all intelligible for an experienced eye; in which everything has its reason to be where it is.[31] This statement was strikingly similar to the later axiom of the "house-machine." "House-machine" designated an architectural object that, like a machine, possesses various components that relate to one another through analysis and economy of selection. According to Le Corbusier, "If we eliminate from our hearts and minds all dead concepts in regard to the house, and look at the question from a critical and objective point of view, we shall arrive at the 'house-machine.' "[32]

Dom-i-no is probably the most prominent manifesto of the modern attitude toward nature, technology, and cultural life. It is indeed an architectonic response to the new techniques and materials that had been used in engineering for some time. While Le Corbusier praised the beauty of the results of engineers' work, he nevertheless stressed that architecture must go beyond such works and create its own aesthetics. He achieved this transcendence but paid a high price for it by creating an architecture obsessed with painting.[33] Le Corbusier's practice and writing exhibit the displacement of ideas, themes, and metaphors from vernacular architecture, engineering, and painting. These ideas and themes associated with painting were formative for his architectural discourse.

In this regard, the plan of Villa Savoye is illustrative: approaching the work as though it were canvas, and he, an artist, Le Corbusier produced an abstract architecture by means of collage. Emptying the elements of architecture of their historical dimension, he played successfully with mass and surface to create his object of beauty. To this end, the notion of contour acquires new meaning and recalls Durand's grid. According to Le Corbusier, "contour is free of all constraint": there is no longer "any question of custom, nor of tradition nor of construction nor of adoption to utilitarian needs."[34] Indeed, with the frame of contour, the plan frees itself from the facade, or vice versa, and walls become a skin-like covering. The open plan provides a surface in which line flows to become contour and its geometry creates void. For Le Corbusier, "space is the central problem of purism, whether architectural or pictorial." He adds, "We think of painting not as a surface, but as a space."[35] It is clear that, in his discourse, there is an overlap between architecture and painting, but the latter dominates through his stress on the "regulating lines."

Villa Savoye is also exemplary in terms of its break with the planimetric and aesthetic aspects of the language of classical architecture. The plan exploits the notion of the open plan, a spatial representation of the late-Enlightenment conception of human freedom. The setting back of columns from the edge of the concrete slab is a device that nullifies the vertical datum. The facade itself is "free"; the walls which are no longer load-bearing members, have thus abandoned their historical role of connecting the building to the earth. Indeed, they do not signify "wallness." The structural organs – such as slab, column, and stairway – are clothed with horizontal plane surfaces that windows and other openings penetrate without restriction. Villa Savoye is an abstract artistic creation, an object of new beauty.[36]

POETICS OF TECHNOLOGY

Absent in Gropius's and Le Corbusier's discourse on objectivity is the "real" use of an object type: the usefulness of a thing, not in terms of its mere functionality, but in terms of its response to the culture of building.

This issue was considered by Adolf Loos around 1908 and by Hans Poelzig in 1931. For Loos there exist two object types: objects for use and objets d'art.[37] The latter are semi-autonomous entities that do not have to appeal to anyone, while the former, changing through use, should appeal to everyone.[38] Adhering to this idea of object type, Loos, in criticizing the Werkbund school, pointed out that they were confusing cause-and-effect relationships. He wrote: "We do not sit in a particular way because a carpenter has made a chair in such and such a manner. A carpenter makes a chair in a particular manner because that is how we wish to sit."[39] For Loos, artifacts do not change because of technical imperatives or the process of production. The new materials and techniques so dear to Gropius were only means, according to Loos, to "repeat" the old in a new spirit. This idea of object type was shared by Poelzig. Both Loos and Poelzig also distinguished technological from architectural forms.

Poelzig, in 1931, strongly questioned the "practical reality" of the new objectivity. His skepticism is expressed in his concern that tendencies in the Modern movement that denied ornament had begun to play with construction methods. For Poelzig, technology and its products belonged to the laws of nature, and their validity is due to technological considerations.[40] In this canon, art and technology belong to two distinct spheres. Technology is a product of reason and calculation, a factual means or an object of utility. Art, in contrast, resides in the domain of values, that is, representation.[41] But the Modern movement did not distinguish objects d'art from technical objects. Airships and airplanes were inspirational for Le Corbusier, and Gropius dreamed of the unity of art and technology.

It should be stressed here that there is a strong relationship between art, particularly architecture, and technology. Architecture absorbs technical facts and transforms them into architectural figures. Architectural figures can respond to the emotions and feelings of a given culture of building if architecture alludes to the "same type of dwellings, which have always provoked those feelings in people, in the past."[42] This typological understanding of architecture is amplified by Poelzig when he recalls Paul Valéry's *Eupalinos*.[43] In a dialogue between Socrates and Phaidros, the latter characterized architecture as a monument that speaks or at best sings, not to nature or to the world of the machine, but to the people of a place. The medium of such orchestration is the "culture of building" – that is, *"techne."*

According to Martin Heidegger, *techne* is the Greek word for technology. In a very existentialist sense, Heidegger considered *techne* both "poetic and revealing."[44] In this paradox, *techne* not only designates tools and fabrication, but signifies, primarily, its place in the world of values, that is, "knowing."[45] This "knowing" is not positivistic. Technology draws only from its own resources, – physics and mechanics – while *techne* precedes practical knowledge and resides in parts, in poetics. For Heidegger, the acts of craftspersons, like those of artists, are poetic insofar as these acts bring something forth: "whatever passes beyond the nonpresent and goes forward into presencing. . . ."[46] But *techne* is also "revealing," meaning that it makes something palpable according to knowledge of something that has precedent, something that is "the same" as the thing to be made. In this sense, to build a roof refers not to the act of building, but to the roof itself. Thus, *techne* characterizes the ontological relationship between object type and its logos of making.

In architectural discourse, Heidegger's understanding of *techne* can be defined as inclusive of both "tectonic" and "type." The meaning of the tectonic goes beyond construction. It denotes the making of architectonic elements – such as wall, column, beam, and roof – by figurative objectification. Construction is simply a response to gravity: architectural elements are put together with the help of mathematics and mechanics. In the tectonic, column, wall, beam, and roof surpass their structural rationality and reveal meaning. Therefore, the tectonic responds to gravity by analogy rather than "efficiency" or "adequacy." In this context, ornament is not a crime, but a necessity. With the help of detail, ornament acts much like clothing. To this end, classical architecture is unique: in its detailing, ornament becomes integrated with constructional rules through the interplay of revealing and concealing. Therefore, it can be inferred that between the structural utility of architectonic elements and their analogical representation, there is a "void," so to speak, where the tectonic resides. This void molds architectural knowledge, that is, the logos of making. Nevertheless, it changes with the formation of new concepts and themes in architectural discourse and with the images developed in other construction activities.

The ultimate goal of *techne* is not mere formal representation. Although architecture reveals itself by form, that form possesses a certain particularity. The concept of the tectonic should encompass the other aspect of the culture of building, which is type – that is, a constructional form that endures and remains permanent through the ebb and flow of custom and use. Type is a formal structure in which the knowledge of making an object meets the object itself. Similar to an artifact – say, a basket – an architectural object possesses an "inner formal structure" that evolves by use and production.[47] Nevertheless, this general form attains a particular figuration through technical potentialities and tactile sensibilities of a material. In this process, form transcends its geometrical and functional dimensions and is codified as a basic unit of architectural language. Type represents a state of architectural understanding that surpasses the narrow boundaries of empiricism and touches the deepest layers of history – the domain of memory, where a six-foot-long and three-foot-wide mound formed into a pyramid shaped by a shovel incites us, "and something in us says, someone lies buried here. That is architecture."[48] In the absence of these typological considerations, the most poetic representation of architectural elements would not surpass the picturesqueness of painting or the rigidity of sculpture. Constructional form is the image of what the mind's eye of an architect might see, which, once it is realized, will sing and speak as such.

In the early twentieth century, a positivistic canon of the New Objectivity ended with a body of architectural theories that dispensed with history and type. Even Muthesius's stress on the need to integrate old types with the new social and technical demands were thrown off. Gropius and Le Corbusier optimized the relationship between technology and architecture by reference either to the imperatives of the production line or to the purity of machine products. In both cases, architectural discourse became laden with themes and notions drawn from technology. Technical positivity manipulated the figurative aspects of architecture. The result was reflected in the idea of object type, a model or prototype whose repeatability is a dimension of mass production and whose peculiarity is a function of building types.

Architecture, interpreted in terms of type-tectonic, is a critical tool for understanding the positivistic thinking of the Modern movement and the recent scenographic references to history. The concept of type-tectonic proposes an architecture that is neither abstract and "new," in the terms implied in the discourse of modernism, nor classical as conceived by traditional academicians. By tectonic and type, architecture addresses both history and progress in such a way that neither dominates. Louis Kahn's architecture is the exemplar, for it is a restatement of tradition by new means and materials. Like the notion of eternal return, the concept of type-tectonic has the ability to objectify the same in the different.

CHAPTER 3

ADOLF LOOS

The Awakening Moments of Tradition in Modern Architecture

Corresponding in the collective consciousness to the forms of the new means of production, which at first were still dominated by the old (Marx), are images in which the new is intermingled with the old.[1]

Benjamin's statement is at the heart of his thought on the idea of the "dialectical image." Writing about the arcades of Paris, Benjamin remarked that the dialectical image "refers to the use of archaic images to identify what is historically new about the nature of commodities."[2] What is notable here is Benjamin's contention that in order to surpass the limits of historicism, one should think of the present according to the index of the claims of the past, a point of view whose theoretical horizon, I would suggest, goes beyond the mainstream of the architecture of the 1920s. In one way or another, modern architecture was concerned with the architectonic implications of the "spirit of time" and its autonomy from the historical past. Le Corbusier's ideas in *Towards a New Architecture* and De Stijl's constructs are works whose conflict with tradition overshadowed their differences and engendered the homogeneous interpretation of contemporary architecture that became known as the Modern movement.

However, between the nineteenth century's urban development and Benjamin's unique observation there stands the work of Adolf Loos and his critical position on tradition. Where Le Corbusier's analogy between a Greek temple and an automobile ended in abstract formal aesthetics, Loos's oeuvre recalls certain aspects of the tradition of dwelling rather than the emerging conditions of modern life. And while the Bauhaus's obsession with the dichotomy between art and technology aligned architecture with the production line, one notices in Loos's work a reserved interest in technology.

Loos's Steiner House provides a case in point, illustrating
his discourse on tradition – first, in terms of its typological
reinterpretation and, second, in regard to his distinction
between the tactile and aesthetic aspects of the interiors of
his houses. These two points reveal Loos's belief that there is
no alternative but to think and design for both the reality of
modern life and the lasting qualities of the tradition of
dwelling. [3]

The early nineteenth century's sociocultural and economic
development shook the unified totality of the preindustrial
society. The incursion of trains into the cities and the architecture of railroad stations and arcades not only punctuated
the homogenous facades of the cities, [4] but more important,
transformed the traditional homology between private and
public spaces. The spatial configuration of arcades presented
a visual montage of the past and present and opened a new
horizon where the light from the skylights illuminated a
place in which every object could be seen as a commodity.
Even the human body became a potential purchase: the figures of prostitutes were displayed in the passages, like "icons
in niches." The flaneur, strolling among the crowd, could
not recall the bygone feeling of "home" but became lost in
his character of alienated object. The emerging contrast between the rapid transformation of urban life and the traditional fabric of the cities might be associated with the
awakening moments of a sleeper, that still moment when a
dream crystallizes into reality. Seeing this transformation,
one can argue that Loos's interiors were conceived as a place
of retreat from the shocking alterations in the public realm.

The duality between modernity and tradition can be traced
back to the quarrel between the ancients and the moderns. [5] It
is also expressed in contemporary artistic work, for example,
in Beethoven's symphonies, where the joy of redemption
was anchored to a strong feeling of belonging, or in Henri
Rousseau's paintings, where primitive figures were juxta-
posed with a technique that anticipated Dadaism and Cubism. Beyond the dreamlike quality of these works, it was
Benjamin's "angel of history" that could unfold the awakening potentialities of the objects of the "new nature":

A Paul Klee painting named Angelus Novus shows an angel looking as though he is about to move away from something he is fix-
edly contemplating. . . . The angel would like to stay, awaken the
dead, and make whole what has been smashed. But a storm is
blowing from the paradise; it has got caught in his wings with such
violence that the angel can no longer close them. This storm irre-

Figure 7. Adolf Loos,
Looshaus, Michaelerplatz,
Vienna, 1909–11, overall
view. From Benedetto
Gravagnuolo, *Adolf Loos,
"Teoria e opere"* (Milan:
Idea Books, 1982).

sistibly propels him into the future to which his back is turned,
while the pile of debris before him grows skyward. This storm is
what we call progress.[6]

Benjamin's thought is suggestive mainly because of its affirmative and yet nonpositivistic interpretation of "progress."
Here, progress is seen from a perspective whose vanishing
point is fixed in the present, while its principle of construction is montage. This perspectival reversal entails a different
understanding of the relationship between past and present.
For Benjamin, what was "new" in contemporary urban life
was the ability to recollect tradition in a secularized mode.
Loos's work may be presented as the architectonic expression
of Benjamin's esteem for the poetic dimension of the process
of secularization of cultural values. This aspect of Loos's
work is implied in his exclusion of architecture from the
realm of art and its confinement to the architecture of tomb
and monument.[7]

The idea of dialectical image also achieves architectural
form in the Looshaus, built in 1910 (Figure 7). The Looshaus
is Loos's most complex and controversial work. Benedetto
Gravagnuolo has done an in-depth analysis of this building;[8]
my interest here is to demonstrate the importance of the con-

cept of montage as it has been utilized by Loos – first, for the massing of the Looshaus and, second, in its relation to the Michaelerplatz. The tripartite composition of the Looshaus might be associated with the language of the classical order. But in addition to this anthropocentric analogy, one might point to Loos's interest in the metaphoric operation of form and material and their life in memory. The stone of the non-load-bearing columns of the ground floor and the space between these columns and the entrance window speak of a public architecture derived from classical tradition. It is to Loos's credit that he thinks of marble not merely in terms of its material reality but in what Demetri Porphyrios has called the "stylistic density" – that is, "the coded meanings that classicism has already assigned to it."[9] It seems that Loos was aware of this aspect of his work when he suggested that "not just the material, but the forms as well are bound up with place, with the nature of the earth and of the air." Meanwhile, as Gravagnuolo reminds us, the curve of the original windows of the entrance follows the form of the square, linking the Looshaus to it (Figure 8). This configuration also completes the overall form of the Michaelerplatz itself. The lime wash of its roof, however, connects the building "with the history of the city of Vienna as a whole."[10] The upper four stories, with windows identical both in shape and size and their plaster finishing, denote formal and tactile aspects of traditional dwellings. By juxtaposing elements from local and classical traditions, Loos denies any possibility of a homogenous architectural language within the modern city. In fact, it was the dreamlike image of the Looshaus that incited such violent public disapproval of it. Cartoons of the building are ironical and very apt (Figures 9 and 10). They depict the Looshaus either with a figure of an aristocrat whose appearance recalls the classical temperament of the ground floor or else with a passerby staring at a street manhole, referring to the austere and rational character of the upper stories. Nevertheless, Loos's design affirms that the technique of montage is a principle of the construction of new typologies from the fragments of the culture of building. This last point vindicates the following reading of the Steiner House.

The Steiner House embodies the idea of montage in the dialectics of its inside–outside spaces and its front–rear elevations (Figure 11). To present an urban image of the house, Loos perceives the interior as the opposite of the exterior: "The building should be dumb on the outside and reveal its wealth only on the inside."[11] The sober and simple facades of

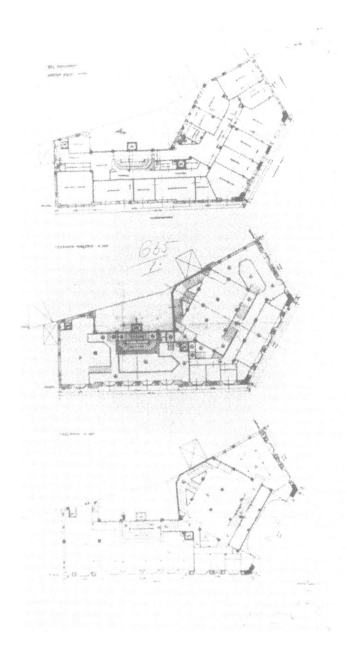

Figure 8. Adolf Loos,
Looshaus, Michaelerplatz,
Vienna, 1909–11, plan.
From Benedetto
Gravagnuolo, *Adolf Loos,
"Teoria e opere"* (Milan:
Idea Books, 1982).

Loos's houses dissociate his discourse from classical language in favor of the archaic and vernacular ethos of the house. Loos's belief that the interior of the house should conform to the dweller's lived experience recollects the vernacular understanding of the house as a useful cultural product. "Every piece of furniture, every thing, every object had a story to tell, a family history," said Loos of his parent's house. And he continues: "The house was never finished; it grew along

47

with us and we grew within it. Of course it did not have any style to it. But there was one style that our house did have – the style of its occupant, the style of our family."[12] These lines could be associated with Benjamin's concept of "the authenticity of an artifact," whose aura, that is, uniqueness, is legitimized by the infusion of sociocultural and technical values into an artifact.[13] In this context, a house is conceived as a sign, a cultural artifact in which the syntax of its architectural elements is codified and its use is identified collectively. Yet Loos was quick to discern and confirm the differences between the use-value character of the traditional house and its spatial and economic commodification: "There is always a spiritual bond between the producer and the consumer of goods," Loos maintained, but "it surely cannot be extended to rooms that are for living."[14] If this implied distinction between inside and outside – where the inside still maintains certain tactile and visual aspects of the traditional dwelling – is extended to the spatial organization of a metropolis, then one might suggest that Loos's understanding of the relationship between interior and exterior is driven by the dichotomy between culture and technology. This dichotomy is also a filter to accelerate the process of secularization of spiritual values by and under the spell of the laws of commodity production. Loos's concern for the duality of inside–outside also discloses an awareness of the disintegration of preindustrial culture and its impact on the body. One thinks of George Simmel's observation that in the Metropolis the individual "has become a mere cog in an enormous organization of things and powers which tear from his hand all progress,

Figure 9. A contemporary cartoon of the Looshaus. From Benedetto Gravagnuolo, *Adolf Loos, "Teoria e opere"* (Milan; Idea Books, 1982).

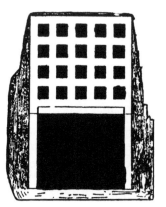

Figure 10. A 1911 cartoon of the Looshaus facade. From Hermann Czech and Wolfgang Mistelbauer, *Das Looshaus* (Vienna Locker & Wogenstein, 1976).

48

spirituality, and value in order to transform their subjective life."[15] In this metamorphosis, Loos perceived the interior as a place of comfort where a person could recollect a bygone subjective spirituality, even in the short periods of recuperation. Besides evincing a strong sense of intimacy and warmth, the presence of fireplaces, exposed wooden beams, and extensive use of wood in Loos's early houses acknowledge his concern for the rift between culture and civilization,[16] as well as the idea of dressing, a critical concept for his theory of architecture that I will discuss shortly.

The import of the idea of montage in the Steiner House should also be understood in light of Loos's typological transformation. The overall massing of the Steiner House recalls Baldassare Peruzzi's Villa Farnesina built 1508–10 (Figure 12). Built on a horseshoe-shaped plan with its central loggia flanked by two wings, the Villa Farnesina reinterprets the courtyard palazzo type. The main entrance is centered in the loggia, whose garden front contains a simple straight wall with a door opening on the garden. A similar disposition of the garden side and the main entrance is at work in the Steiner House. The major differences between these two buildings, of course, reside in their "language" and the spatial organization of their interiors, not to mention their differences in scale. Moreover, while the one remains restricted to the Renaissance concern for mathematical distribution of

Figure 11. Adolf Loos, Steiner House, Vienna, 1910. From Benedetto Gravagnuolo, *Adolf Loos, "Teoria e opere"* (Milan, Idea Books, 1982).

the space, the other transcends such a normative approach
and suggests a purposeful arrangement of the interior space
in the manner of what has been called the *Raumplan*. I will
come back to this subject later, but a comprehensive typological analysis of these two buildings would not do them justice
unless Karl Friedrich Schinkel's design for an urban residence
in Berlin were mentioned (Figure 13).

Simplified elevations, the appropriation of the courtyard
type for an urban fabric, and the strategic intention to transform the sectional organization of the house are characteristic
of both Schinkel's and Loos's Steiner House designs. The
courtyard, in its conventional form, is usually considered a
private space. However, Schinkel put the courtyard at the
front of the house and elevated it onto the *piano nobile* forming a terrace overlooking the street.

But Loos's intervention is even more radical than Schinkel's. First, the Steiner House dispenses with the central
courtyard; second, it reduces the loggia – an important architectonic element for both Peruzzi and Schinkel – to a projection appearing in front of the first floor of the central part
of the main facade.

In terms of material and tactile sensibilities, Loos again departs from the point where Schinkel's and Peruzzi's vision
ended. The facade of the Villa Farnesina was strictly perceived within the Renaissance language of representation
embedded in Leon Battista Alberti's analogy between architecture and the body. Schinkel presented an abstract interpretation of that language. He dismissed Alberti's discourse on
column and wall and sees the logos of making in terms of
Roman architecture. The stratification of his elevations embodies the constructional function of the wall that is common in Roman architecture. In contrast, the facades of the
Villa Farnesina recall Alberti's idea of lineaments, that is,
the aesthetic articulation of the exterior wall with non-load-
bearing columns, punctuated by the smooth finish of the
main wall, visible between the columns. Again Loos's position is more complex than that of his predecessors. He presents an abstract interpretation of both the Roman wall and
Alberti's analogy of building as body. The notion of dressing, which is "the oldest architectural detail,"[17] is key to
Loos's aesthetic operation. The unornamented plaster walls
of the Steiner House cover the body of the building in a manner that leaves no room for representation and resemblance.
The idea of dressing differs from the Renaissance stratification of the facade in that the latter aimed to make the rusti-

Figure 12. Baldassare
Peruzzi, Villa Farnesina,
Rome, 1508–10. From
Christian Norberg-Schulz,
*Meaning in Western
Architecture* (New York:
Rizzoli International
Publications, 1980).

Figure 13. Karl Friedrich
Schinkel, Urban Residence
project. From Karl
Friedrich Schinkel,
*Collection of Architectural
Designs* (Princeton, N.J.:
Princeton Architectural
Press, 1989).

cated base different from both the nonsupportive and decorative columns and pilasters laid over the wall of the *piano nobile*. Loos's understanding of dressing also differs from the Secessionist obsession with appearance; they esteemed ornamentation of the body of the building from one end to the other and from corner to parapet, generating the feeling that the wall was not solidly constructed. Loos's idea of dressing recalls Gottfried Semper's *Bekleidung*. In his distinction between the core-form and the art-form, Semper suggests that in early civilizations the interior space was surrounded by carpets hung from a frame that fulfilled the structural and practical needs of space making. According to him, the carpet was later conceived as a stylistic or tectonic surrogate for dressing a masonry spatial enclosure – the solid structure of which, as Loos would put it, was secondary. Nevertheless, Loos's reflections on *Bekleidung* should be read in the context of the dichotomy between culture and civilization: the interiors of his houses are "dressed" according to the practical and psychological needs of domesticity. Yet the simple and at times fragmented exteriors are never reduced to a "dress,"[18] either for stylistic or ornamental purposes. Affirming the solidity of the built volume, however, the Steiner House's white-finished exterior recalls the tradition of both Viennese dwellings and the whitewashed facades of Mediterranean vernacular architecture.

In addition to its aesthetic considerations, Loos's interpretation of tradition discloses a theoretical horizon different from that of his contemporaries. His typological transformation is not arbitrary, and it does not reflect the *Zeitgeist*. He believed that one must build in the same way that the Romans did. Yet he never held dogmatically to the cultural values of the past, in lieu of modernization, nor did he embrace technical innovations blindly. Rather, alone among his contemporaries, Loos produced an architecture that not only "preserves tradition, but also, to a degree, deprives it of its content."[19] As already mentioned, in his article entitled "Architecture" Loos distinguishes architecture from the work of art and asserts that "a house should appeal to everybody, as distinct from works of art, which do not have to appeal to any one." And he continues: "The work of art aims at shattering men's comfortable complacency. A house must serve one's comfort."[20] These words are suggestive of the present concern over "the death of architecture"; has Loos accepted the idea that architecture has no radical role in bringing about social transformation? Behind and within his "conformist" veil, Loos houses the psychological and emotional world in the spatial organization of the *Raumplan*. If this is a plausible reading of Loos, then there are important implications for architecture and its interaction with culture and civilization, as well as for the relationship between form and technique.

This proposition is suggestive of the concept of the *Raumplan*, a system of spatial displacement that disintegrates the sectional organization of the interior space. Simultaneity of space and time maps a perceptual horizon where functional distribution of space is not confined within four walls and two parallel slabs. Starting with the Steiner House, Loos bases his planimetric organization on the technique of cutting and sliding different floors over each other. The elision serves, according to Kenneth Frampton, "not only to create spatial movement but also to differentiate one living area from the next."[21]

Reading the concept of the *Raumplan*, one cannot dismiss the importance of the stair in Loos's plans. Losing its monumentality, the stair is turned into an architectonic element of incision; the stair deconstructs the Platonic concept of a uniform space as it is represented in the two-dimensional nature of a flat plan.

The possibility of conceiving a separation between the structural and non-load-bearing members is critical for any transformation of the sectional organization of a space. The independence of the plan from the facade is also important to this technical consideration. Of these technical aspects of the *Raumplan*, Loos had nothing specific to say. It was left to Le Corbusier to unfold the aesthetic and formal implications of the new building technology with the ideas of Dom-i-no and *plan libre* as a postscript to the *Raumplan*. Stanislaus von Moos has recently addressed the difference between these two design strategies.[22] Le Corbusier's and Loos's criticisms of the Bauhaus and the Viennese Secessionists is crucial to von Moos's argument. To his credit, he recognizes the difference between the Moller House and Maison Planix – both built around 1927 – in terms of the impact of new material and building techniques on their architectonic images. It is also the case that the dissimilarities between these two projects are not derived from their authors' reflections on technical issues, but from their divergent approach to architectural tradition. A comparison of the utilization of loggia in the Tzara House and the Villa Stein will support this reading. While the Villa Stein represents an abstract image of the loggia, Loos reinterprets this architectonic element within the culture of building. For Le Corbusier, however, the *plan libre* and the free facade distill the tradition of building, as he explicitly stated in his five points. For Loos, every design, from the curved roof of the Steiner House to the metal barrel roof of the Horner House, is an occasion to recollect local and classical themes.

As noted earlier, the cultural content of Loos's typological transformations is the main point of Frampton's observation. He sees Loos's formulation of the *Raumplan* as an "architectural strategy for transcending the contradictory cultural legacy of bourgeois society which, having deprived itself of the vernacular, could not claim in exchange the culture of classicism."[23] Does the concept of the *Raumplan* assist the bourgeoisie in resolving its cultural dilemma? A positive response to this question would not secure a conservative position for Loos as an advocate for the secularization of architecture. Once again, in order to assess Loos's radical nihilism, we might recall his discourse on the dialectic of inside–outside. It is true that the white-finished exterior of the Steiner House anticipates the death of architecture and the silence of the culture industry. Yet it is also true that the interiors of his houses provided a chance, perhaps the last, for the lived tradition to evolve. For the duality of modernity and tradition to persist, a particular intellectual caliber, of the kind Loos has expressed in his writing and building, was needed. He never resigned himself to or became assimilated into the cultural power of the status quo; instead, he presented his oeuvre as an alternative to it.

Loos's thought suggests the intellectual utilization of the technique of montage, a kind of critical inquiry that, in light of Gianni Vattimo's thought on secularization, one could only expect from "weak thought," a discourse that approaches the question of the beginning, as opposed to both Hegelian historicism and the metaphysical framework, which always return to the first principles of being. According to Vattimo, this third way presumes a concept of "experience" that remains faithful to the "already given and everyday, which is always historically qualified and culturally dense."[24] His entry for the Chicago Tribune Building competition is worth mentioning as a case in point. Against postmodern jubilant interpretation of this project as a major note in the swan song of current eclecticism, Loos's recollection of the classical column reminds us of the scope of possibilities that "weak thought" might unfold as we attempt to register a different meaning for architecture. And, of course, it reveals the dreamlike quality of the wakening moments of tradition in light of the modernity of the mid-twenties.

CHAPTER 4

MÉTIER

*Frank Lloyd Wright's Tradition
of Dwelling*

I deliberately chose to break with tradition in order to be more true to tradition than current conventions and ideals in architecture would permit.[1]

In the words "tradition" and "dwelling," one could read the nonwritten, romantic quest for bygone days. If we continued in this vein, we might associate the yearning of the Arts and Crafts movement for the "cottage," a building that uses traditional materials and techniques and is infused with its natural context. Philip Webb's Red House represents the architectural manifestation of this convention. In consideration of the space opened up by a negative attitude toward modernity, a nontransient view of tradition was inevitable. However, the Arts and Crafts movement's concern for tradition does have merit. It presents an awareness concerning the process of liquidation of traditional values through secularization. In other words, the advocates of the Arts and Crafts movement could see what Walter Benjamin later called the loss of aura – the distance that mechanization introduces between tradition and reproduced artifact.[2] But by locating tradition in the aura of craftsmanship and perceiving the idea of dwelling in the cottage, the Arts and Crafts movement stopped short of distancing itself from nineteenth-century historicism. English picturesque architecture and its later migration to the United States, under the rubric of the "Queen Anne" style, characterizes the main aspect of a nostalgic view of the aura of dwelling. Indigenous architecture was considered to be the genesis of tradition.

T. S. Eliot, writing in 1919, averred that in order to overcome the distance between the past and the present, we need to conceptualize a "historical sense." Eliot conceded that this involves a "sense of the timeless as well as of the temporal and of the timeless and of the temporal together."[3] To accept the loss of the aura and maintain a transient concept of tradition, we must look beyond nineteenth-century historicism. In his 1910 article "Architecture," while praising the profound beauty and tranquility of a mountain lake setting, Adolf Loos framed the following picture of an indigenous and modern dwelling:

the loss of the aura and maintain a transient concept of tradition, we must look beyond nineteenth-century historicism. In his 1910 article "Architecture," while praising the profound beauty and tranquility of a mountain lake setting, Adolf Loos framed the following picture of an indigenous and modern dwelling:

Ah, what is that? A false note in this harmony. Like an unwelcome scream. In the center, beneath the peasants' homes which were created not by them but by God, stands a villa. Is it the product of a good or a bad architect? I do not know. I only know that peace, tranquility and beauty are no more.[4]

The picture Loos painted of an early settlement does not represent a romantic view of nature, which is an essential component of any analysis of the primitive elements of architecture. However, Loos was concerned with contemporary architecture and its relationship with the tradition of dwelling and with the way in which one experiences architectonic elements in association with the tactile and emotive dimensions of the body. Loos's discourse on the tradition of dwelling is partially motivated by Gottfried Semper's ideas on "dressing" and treatment of material. Yet in his architecture, Loos utilized the architectonic aspects of both classical and vernacular tradition. Certainly Loos unfolds and invigorates Semper's ideas in the phrase: "how to change old forms, consecrated by necessity and tradition according to our new means of fabrication."[5] By emphasizing métier – that is, the historically shared techniques – Semper initiated a different discourse on tradition that surpasses the nostalgic and historicist view of the Arts and Crafts movement.

It is my belief that Wright, on the periphery of European intellectual trends, provided a new momentum for Semper's discourse on métier. Wright's allusion to tradition is not conservatorial, as Smith Norris Kelly assumes,[6] but rigorous in the sense that it might be associated with some aspects of European realist architecture of the turn of the century, especially the latter's regional content.[7] In fact, there are more thematic affinities between Wright and Loos, as the heir of that tradition, than between Wright and the "new pioneers" of the Modern movement. This dimension of Wright's work is neglected by contemporary architectural historiography. In fact, it is this aspect of Wright's architecture that made the curators of the "international style" associate him with Peter Behrens, August Perret, and Van de Veld, while having difficulty making room for Wright's work in the MOMA's

exhibition.[8] Furthermore, Wright's remarks on tradition
suggest that he was aware of the ways he differed from his
contemporaries, who either sought tradition in opposition to
the "new" or conceived it in the ossified forms of history.

Standing aside from both eclecticism and the international
style of his period, Wright let some aspects of tradition "pass
on situations, by making them practicable and thus liquidat-
ing them."[9] Moreover, in his planimetric and aesthetic organization, Wright revealed a metaphoric discourse in which
"what is transmitted by tradition is not things, and least of all
monuments, but situations – not solitary artifacts but the
strategies that construct and mobilize them."[10] Wright's
main strategy lay in archaic impulse, the feeling for archaic
principle valid then and thereafter. All of Wright's work
demonstrated his interest in the existential depth of the relationship between being and place. For him, architecture "is
man in possession of his earth."[11] Like that of Semper,
Wright's design economy put emphasis on the universal
ethos of the tradition of dwelling, that is, the roof and the
hearth, as well as dressing and axial composition. Yet
Wright's dichotomous approach to tradition suggests a
"heterotopic"[12] language that draws its formative concepts
from classicism and from vernacular and modern discourse
without sustaining their textual power. It is this heterotopic
sensibility that allows one to pursue the idea of montage in
Wright's constructs and in his planimetric organization, by
which he brings together fragments of different architectonic
expressions without commanding a unified language.

From 1893 to 1910, Wright set down a metaphoric language known as Prairie architecture. What distinguishes this
period from the rest of Wright's career is the attempt he
makes to restate tradition by new means and materials. Unlike architects from the Arts and Crafts movement, he never
yearned for the cottage or became obsessed with the power of
classical architecture. His task was of a different kind: he designed and thought both within and outside of the spectrum
of classical and vernacular tradition. As Kelly has observed,
we can find the meaning and nature of Wright's work in this
polar tension.[13] To support this argument, it ought to be
enough to mention the heterotopic nature of Wright's planimetric organization. This design economy was achieved by
the particular utilization of cross-axial composition. Of this
style the Ward Willitts house is exemplary; its cross axis has
the deep structure of a nonhomogenous distribution of space
(Figure 14). In contrast to classical architecture, in Wright's

plan, the cross axis neither sustains frontality nor initiates a symmetrical order. In the Ward Willitts house, Wright summons the basic sensation of place, as if a nomad were experiencing it. In this context, the cross axis is the abstract representation of the natural existence of the earth, a device for orientation, settlement, and departure. It signifies what Le Corbusier would later call the regulating line, a base for construction and satisfaction.[14]

In Wright's plans, the cross axis has a different connotation than it does in Beaux Arts compositions, which view the void in the center according to the vicissitudes of anthropocentric discourse. Wright, in contrast, transcends the humanistic view in favor of an elementary perception of the relationship between being and place in which "every inhabited region has what may be called center; that is a place sacred above all."[15] In almost every plan, the center is given over to the hearth, the fireplace, where the comfort attained through its warmth stimulates a temporary feeling of settlement. One might claim that, described from a distance, the picture of a person sitting by a fire from which smoke rises is the most primitive nonverbal expression of dwelling. Wright strengthens this perception through his cross-axial plans. Is not the heavy masonry chimney soaring above the Robie House's roof symbolic of the integrity of existence and the earth (Figure 15)? Even more than their aesthetic composition, the masonry chimney and the floating roof connote two primitive instincts: one of mobility and the other of security.[16] In the Robie House, Wright makes an attempt to fasten the flying roofs to the earth. However, his later life and architecture re-

Figure 14. Frank Lloyd Wright, Ward Willits House, Highland Park, Illinois, 1900. Photo courtesy of the Frank Lloyd Wright Archives, Taliesin West, Scottsdale, Arizona.

veal that in the culture of "mobocracy," it is difficult, if not impossible, to be with and dwell in a place.

Wright's *parti* of floating roof and masonry chimney suggests other readings. At one level, we are concerned with the particular place of the roof in his discourse. Throughout his writings, Wright expresses a peculiar interest in the etymological aspect of the roof for the awareness of the sense of "home." Here it seems that Wright agreed with Semper that the roof was one of the four major architectonic expressions of the primitive condition of life. This comparison does not dismiss the difference between the two architects: for Semper, the roof was an essential constructive element developed out of carpentry. Obviously, Wright was less concerned with the relationship between the roof and other technical arts. Rather, he saw the roof as an existential component of architecture. According to Wright, "man came to speak of his house as his roof and was fond of inviting strangers to come and sit or stay under his roof. . . . His roof was not only his shelter, it was his dignity, as well as his sense of home."[17]

At another level, our interest lies in Wright's specific formal treatment of the roof. The horizontal dimension reflects the building's "tendency" to be with the earth. Wright believed that the "planes parallel to earth in buildings identify themselves with the ground, make the building belong to the

Figure 15. Frank Lloyd Wright, Robie House, Chicago, 1909. Photograph courtesy of the Frank Lloyd Wright Archives, Taliesin West, Scottsdale, Arizona.

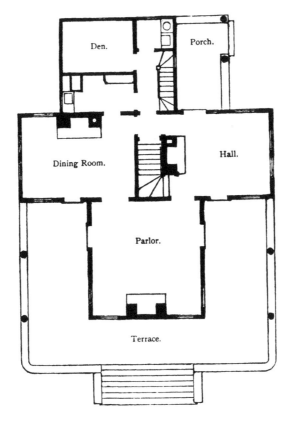

Figure 16. Bruce Price,
Kent House, Tuxedo Park,
New York, 1885–6. From
G. W. Sheldon, *Artistic
Country Seats* (New York:
Appleton, 1886).

ground."[18] Throughout his early and late buildings, Wright recollected the archaic sense of place in which attention to the sky is offset with horizontal vision. This esteem for horizontality is magnified by an attempt to break down the boxlike character of a room.

The desire to transcend the rigid order of the classical plan can be traced in other examples of American domestic architecture as well. Bruce Price's plan for the Kent House is one of the earliest moves in this direction (Figure 16). Wright restates this typology in his Coonly Playhouse. But in the Willitts House, and later in the Robie House, he went beyond Price's experience. In both of these houses, Wright dismantled the formal coherency of the classical composition. The emphasis on the hearth is dialectically strengthened with a sense of dispersion, which extends even beyond its functional domain. The wall, relieved from the burden of aesthetic connotations, looks for another kind of order: "A kind of natural integrity – the integrity of each in all and of all in each."[19] Wright's planimetric organization can be read as a response to the "desire" of the building to stretch itself along the earth in order to maximize its belonging and attachment to it. In this regard, the Martin House is exemplary (Figure 17); the plan challenges the rationale of the wall, and in return the plan is disrupted by the brick wall running horizontaly around the building. Wright's design technique discloses a complex perception of enclosure; it displays some aspects of both column and wall. At the same time, it does not represent either in its totality. And the rigid barrier dividing the inside from the outside was also surpassed. The inside is seen as part of the outside, and both as part of the landscape.[20] One might conclude that the plan of the Martin House recalls the primitive sense of place defined by stone hedges.

The heterotopic character of Wright's architecture was not confined to his planimetric organization. It operated also in Wright's aesthetic valorization and material treatment, the language of which might be traced in both classical and vernacular tradition. In the Winslow House, designed as early as 1893, the street facade is discernible from the garden side by its strict compositional order (Figure 18). The cornice running around the building and the change of material above counter the concept of the wall as a coherent structural or aesthetic entity. This interruption expresses the tectonic of a wooden frame dressed with brick. The tripartite compositional order dominant in the street elevation of this house is a

Figure 17. Frank Lloyd Wright, Martin House, Buffalo, New York, 1904, plan. Courtesy of the Frank Lloyd Wright Archives, Taliesin West, Scottsdale, Arizona.

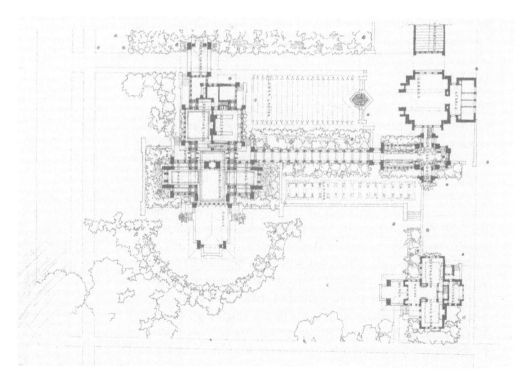

Figure 18. Frank Lloyd Wright, Winslow House, River Forest, Illinois, 1893, front and rear views. Photographs courtesy of the Frank Lloyd Wright Archives, Taliesin West, Scottsdale, Arizona.

montage of a Sullivanesque entrance, classical norms of aesthetic valorization, and a roof that speaks for vernacular dwelling. The roof, the frieze below it – which is the extension of the main structural frame – and the brick enclosure could be perceived as three spatial constructs held together by montage.[21] One can claim that Wright's design economy operates outside the morality of craftsmanship and the language of classical architecture; his work is suggestive of a mode of thinking and making that operates beyond a normative technique or a codified stylistic language.

The notion of plasticity is critical for understanding Wright's tectonic figuration. According to Wright, "Plasticity implies total absence of constructed effects as evident in the result. . . . This means that the quality and nature of material are seen flowing or growing into form instead of seen as built up out of a cut and joined process."[22] This statement adheres to the principle of dressing and expresses a formal sensibility integral to the given material. Loos's idea of dressing – the oldest architectural detail – is a commentary on Semper's *Bekleidung,* by which he discusses the metamorphosis of the early wall-mate into the architectonic of masonry enclosure. Following Semper, Loos asserts that the dressing is the first aspect of architecture, and the structural nature of the wall comes later.[23] The idea of dressing is vividly operative in the elevation of the Ward Willits House. The wooden window stripes are extended to cover the joints of stucco while analogously suggesting the frame beneath.[24] With the change of material, Wright would unfold a different design economy in order to achieve the desired plasticity. In the Unity Temple, the four heavy concrete pillars standing apart from the enclosure speak of a tectonic figuration that rejects a direct expression of the structural elements in the final form (Figure 19). Here, "plasticity may be seen in the expressive flesh-covering of the skeleton as contrasted with the tradition of the skeleton itself."[25] Of course, this does not imply that Wright disliked the new building technology. In his Princeton lectures of 1930, Wright explicitly emphasized the significance of the machine in the poetics of architecture. However, in his designs, Wright strove for an analogous relationship between structural rationality and the expressive aspect of form.

Wright's conception of plasticity did not question the qualitative aspects of material. His insistence on seeing brick as brick and concrete as concrete went beyond the morality of craftsmanship. The latter operates within rules and repetitive

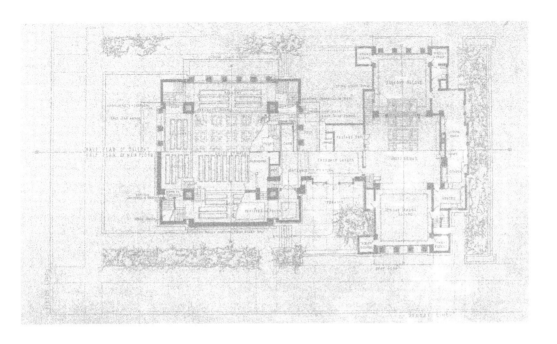

Figure 19. Frank Lloyd Wright, Unity Temple, Oak Park, Illinois, 1906, plan and street view. Photographs courtesy of the Frank Lloyd Wright Archives, Taliesin West, Scottsdale, Arizona.

norms. Wright refused to distinguish matter from form. However, his formal images surpassed the traditional norms and inclined toward difference. The complexity of Wright's perceptual world rested in the space between constructional form and its tectonic figuration. The "lily pad" concrete columns of the Johnson Wax Building and Florida Southern College exhaust functional aspects of form and challenge the forces of gravity. Wright's tectonic figuration attained a critical dimension in the Unitarian Church. The front window follows the slope of the site and evinces the feeling that it is about to shrink. As I mentioned earlier, for Wright, the so-called nature of material was neither a generalized abstraction nor an entity whose quality emerges from actual and habitual use. Each material came to express itself in association with another. In the Unitarian Church, the peculiar juxtaposition of glass and stone implied the fragile quality of the first against the hardness of the other. The same attitude was at work in the design of windows. Windows in Wright's buildings create an intricate dialogue between glass and metal. He exploited the formal potentialities of these two materials to the extent that the glass became subordinate to the metal plate.

Wright's material sensibility convinces us to assert that his architecture was not reducible to the abstract purity of the international style, nor was his tectonic figuration comparable to the picturesqueness of eclecticism. Beyond the spirit of his time, that is, *Zeitgeist,* Wright created formal images in a different architectural language. In Wright's architecture, "Language is no longer the organization of the continuity of nature in relationship to constructed space, but is the instrument that preserves the memory of ancestral civilization by holding their archetypes up to our view again."[26] Wright's formal images are the result of a radical transformation of primeval elements of architecture. In this inversion, he transcended the historicity of form and expressed a transient understanding of tradition. In the polar tension between the now and the dormant past, Wright's tectonic figurations stand as fantasia,[27] a poetic wisdom that narrates the polar opposition of modernity and tradition dialogically.

Now, following Giambattista Vico, we might argue that the art of thinking of particulars in universal forms is the essence of métier. However, in this context one might associate Wright's work with certain aspects of Semper's thought. Wright acknowledges this by recollecting the hearth, the roof, and the principle of dressing. In utilizing these primeval elements, Wright establishes a nonrepresentational and formalistic architecture. His work distills history and gives new birth to the universal ethos of dwelling. However, Wright's power of imagination does not end in abstraction, but leads to a particular signification.[28] His metaphoric language posits architecture in the concrete condition of life. From Chicago to California and to Japan, Wright formulates the thematics of regionalism.[29] Overhangs and garden terraces of the Middle West are as convincingly local as are the bleached planes and boxy wood frames of Taliesin West on the Arizona desert."[30] But the Prairie houses express Wright's dilemma of dwelling in his native land, that is, the original desire of the early immigrant for settlement set against the urge of mobility that was later enforced by the culture industry.

Finally, referring to Wright's position on tradition, we might conclude that his dichotomous attitude unfolds its critical depth in his last work. The heterotopic character of the Guggenheim Museum suggests that the force of the Metropolis urged him to accept the loss of aura. Here, the hearth, the dominant element of the Prairie period, loses its sacred nature. This transformation takes place in the space opened up before the two poles of civilization and tradition. One is symbolized in the mechanical move of the elevators, the other in the circular continuity of the ramp. Moving along the spiraling path and viewing the artwork on the wall, we are haunted by the collective unconscious memory of cave paintings. Nevertheless, this feeling dissipates by the time we arrive at the ground floor, where the center neither invokes the anthropocentric tale nor sustains its formal strength as it does in the Prairie houses. The warmth of the fire is gone and with it the drive for dispersion. Wright emphasizes this lacuna by pushing the fountain area away from the center and locating it next to the ramp. The set is complete and dramatized by the light pouring in from the skylight. This time, light is not the messenger of reason; instead, it baptizes heterotopia as the language through which one "recollects" the tradition of dwelling.

CHAPTER 5

MIES VAN DER ROHE

The Genealogy of Column and Wall

Since the sixties, Mies has been a target of criticism from both the conservative and radical sectors of postmodern architecture. Robert Venturi's motto "Less is bore" and Stanley Tigerman's photomontage depicting the Crown Hall sinking into Lake Michigan show that these two extreme reflections on Mies are part of the general frustration of a postmodernity facing the void that he left. Mies initiated a "minor language," in the Deluzian term of the word,[1] which exhausted the linguistic possibilities of the modern language of architecture to the point that, after Mies, one had no choice but to return to the two major tendencies of modernity: avant-gardism and historicism. This reading of the conditions of postfunctionalist architecture is indeed a Miesian search for the "truth" content of the present state of architecture.

One might locate Mies in "the chain of simplification and obedience to structure" that, according to Colin Rowe, started in the 1870s.[2] This point of view stops short of reflecting on how this esteem for formal simplicity acquired a new nature and magnitude by the first decades of the twentieth century. One might also search beyond the horizon that views Mies's architecture as a reflection of a particular brand of philosophy.[3] Without disregarding these previous assessments, my reading focuses on the themes and concepts by which Mies particularized the project of the historical avant-garde in his architecture.[4] My contention is that Mies debased the metaphoric dimension of architectonic elements in general, and the classical discourse on the relationship between column and wall in particular. By analyzing the syntactical dimensions of Mies's design economy, I wish to discuss the process of demythification of construction and the realization of what I would like to call Mies's speechless art of construction.

In touch with the Berlin avant-garde of his time,[5] Mies set himself the task of decomposing the conventional values of architecture in order to arrive at a new order. Indeed, one might characterize his whole intellectual and professional life as two interrelated poles of disintegration and formation. In his early designs, Mies attempted to deconstruct the architectonic elements of traditional architecture. He believed that in "contrast to the extraordinary order apparent in technical and economic realms, the cultural sphere, moved by no necessity and possessed of no genuine tradition is a chaos of directions, opinions."[6] Thus, to work toward order as a "definition of meaning and measure of being," Mies integrated the universal precision of technology into the domain of culture, and architecture in particular. In so doing, Mies closed the gap between subject (idea) and object (matter).

In a Hegelian sense, Mies conceived of the *Zeitgeist* as a driving force in history infused in and identified with technology. He claimed that "technology is rooted in the past. It dominates the present and tends into the future." Mies believed that the linear progression of technology would surpass its practical dimension to become "something that has meaning and powerful form."[7] This inquiry into the nature of the epoch ended with an inquiry into the intrinsic nature of building art, a point of view that rejects "all aesthetic, all doctrine and all formalism" and restores architecture "to what it should exclusively be: building."[8] Mies's archaizing methodology could be associated with what Paul Ricoeur has called a "hermeneutics of suspicion" – a discourse that looks for the essence of truth under the dust accumulated by the authority of history and the subject's act of "will to form." Mies's archaeology had two consequences. The first was that it caused him to rethink architecture in terms of its constructive elements, devoid of any aesthetic or stylistic intentions imposed from outside. The second was the articulation of the thematics of a building art in which the notion of construction is critical. The genealogy of this architecture can be traced to the process of secularization of the context of the traditional language of architecture. This breakthrough in Mies's work is carried out by a systematic use of modern technology. Nevertheless, from the standpoint of the present, Mies's architecture represents the most eloquent architectural language of steel and glass. Yet Mies is more. One might claim that his architecture anticipated the silence of the culture industry.

From 1919 to 1925, in just a few projects, Mies was already accomplishing certain aspects of his architectural vision. In the Concrete House, the arbitrary appearance of window cuts revealed Mies's plastic sensibility (Figure 20). Besides its dynamic form, which can be associated with some Constructivist compositions, the excessive fenestration helps to break up the traditional cubic house. The continuous ribbon of basement windows separates the building from its site and simulates the cut that a sculptor would make in a bulk of material. Indeed, the entrance to this house displays the act of incision rather than the "gesture" of invitation.

However, by changing the material, Mies would find the proper design device to achieve his objectives. The Brick Country House, designed in 1923, illustrates Mies's treatment of the brick wall (Figure 21). In this design, space is defined and plan is organized by independent walls. The elementarist character of the wall is so compelling that as early as 1934 Alfred Barr did not hesitate to compare its plan to Theo Van Doesburg's painting *Russian Dance*.[9] Beyond their dynamic configurations, both works are exemplary in abstracting their themes. Just as Van Doesburg's painting has, representationally, nothing to do with the reality of dance, so Mies's design hardly relates to any conventional plan of a house. The room as a plan organizer is dissolved and the center is abolished. At one level, the Brick Country House recalls Frank Lloyd Wright's early attempts to break down the boundaries of different rooms. At the level of planimetric organization, the expressive nature of the wall displays a thrust toward one-dimensionality; even the structural raison d'être of the wall is undetermined. The extension of the wall reaches the perceptual domain where a load-bearing mass could be seen as a free-standing plane. One might read these radiating walls as an act integrating the building with its site, or infusing the interior and exterior. Nevertheless, it is the edges of the drawing sheet that bring an end to the prolongation of walls. Here, Mies's perception of the wall recalls the excessive expansion of decoration in Rococo architecture; decorative motives are infused in the frame, undermining its purpose. In this regard, we might assert that Mies's major intention was to dissociate the wall from all its figurative and connotative dimensions until the wall signifies only its matter-of-factness.

Any advance for Mies beyond this stage of abstraction of the wall and nullification of the architectural object would entail a new economy of design. The implementation of the

Figure 20. Mies van der
Rohe, Concrete Country
House project, 1923.
Photograph courtesy of the
Mies van der Rohe
Archive, the Museum of
Modern Art, New York.

Figure 21. Mies van der
Rohe, Brick Country
House project, 1923–4,
plan and perspective.
Photograph courtesy of the
Mies van der Rohe
Archive, the Museum of
Modern Art, New York.

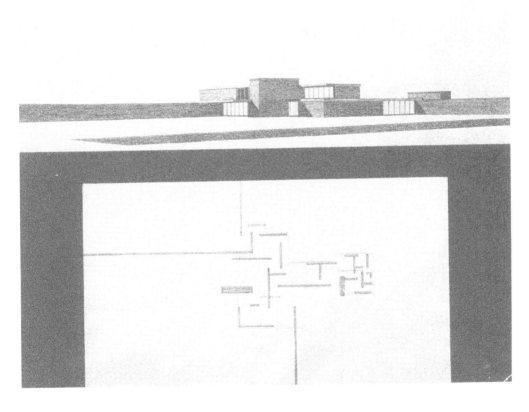

column as formative structural element is strongly stated in the Barcelona Pavilion and the Tugendhat House. In these two houses, walls are reduced to a state of partition, and the plan is stripped of any excessive element. From this point on, Mies unfolds an architectural discourse whose formative concepts are embedded in the dialogical relationships between column and wall. As will be discussed, the interplay of column and wall eventually ended with the total dissolution of the wall and the crystallization of a spatial void through which the body, wrapped in various layers of sheer glass, could experience the silence caused by the absence of any representational intention.

Analyzing the plan of the Pavilion, one notices the compositional motif of a pair of columns standing in front of a wall (Figure 22). It is my belief that this architectonic syntax is the key to unfolding Mies's particular discourse on column and wall. Yet in order to map the genealogy of column and wall in Miesian architecture, it is necessary to examine Leon Battista Alberti's discourse on the column.

The wall is the main structural system of the Renaissance building; however, the column has a major place in Alberti's aesthetic theory. His definition of beauty[10] and his characterization of the column as "the principal ornament in all architecture"[11] might sound contradictory. But in a cultural milieu in which resemblance and similitude are two major forms of knowledge, it would be logical to perceive the col-

Figure 22. Mies van der Rohe, Barcelona Pavilion, 1928, plan. Photograph courtesy of Mies van der Rohe Archive, the Museum of Modern Art, New York.

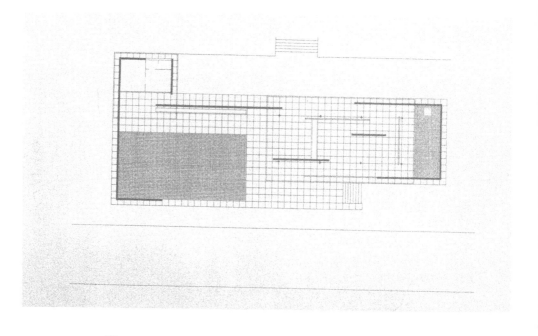

umn in the light of an ornament. Michel Foucault asserts that during the Renaissance the "search for the law governing signs is to discover the signs that are alike."[12] This observation is convincing when we read in Alberti that "a row of columns . . . [is] indeed nothing else but a wall open and discontinued in several places." He adds that "a column is a certain strong continued part of the wall."[13] Alberti's notion of column and wall are discrete and yet identical: one is recognized through the existence of the other (see Figure 1). This dialectical relationship is not rooted in the load-bearing function of column and wall, but stems from their analogical resemblance to a higher order – that is, building understood as body.[14] This semantic context differentiates Alberti's characterization of beam and arch as bones, and ribs as "fillers,"[15] from the Miesian metaphor of "skin and bones." For Alberti, an arch is nothing more than a bent beam, while a transom is only a column laid crosswise. This optimization of architectonic elements is rooted in his perception of the corporeal nature of structure. Mies's vision, in contrast, is more in line with the nineteenth-century functional rationalists. The rationalists, as noted by Hubert Damisch, would see the structure in the discontinuity of its elements, aggregated and based on the efficiency of a load-bearing economy.[16] An architecture structured around the notion of "less is more" attempts to dissociate itself from classical semantic language and identify itself with the factual world of technology.

In Mies's architecture, the relation between column and wall is sustained only in the recognition of their difference. In the Pavilion, the House for a Bachelor, and the Tugendhat House, Mies has reversed Alberti's syntax of column and wall. In these projects, the column stands as a load-bearing element, while the wall displays its liberation, so to speak, from the ordering logic in which column and wall are identical. In Mies's later architecture, walls are no longer subject to the rationality of gravity; rather, they partition the space. Nevertheless, the juxtaposition of column and wall achieves its ultimate complexity in the House for a Bachelor and the Tugendhat House. The semantic depth of this interplay has less to do with the artistic creativity of Mies than with the tectonic bond between these two elements. Therefore, I do not agree with interpretations that attribute the design economy of these projects either to Mies's desire to achieve a higher unity between man and nature or to the creation of a new structural order.[17]

The interplay of column and wall is also the major theme of the planimetric organization of the aforementioned houses. Here, plans are not organized by the taxonomy of functions, but represent one instance among many possible compositions of the Miesian motif of wall and column. In fact, the function of this motif is similar to that of a room in conventional plan organization. In the House for a Bachelor and the Tugendhat House, the wall encloses the dining area, yet it defines the sitting area or the bedroom from other parts. In all these permutations, one thing is consistent and worthy of attention, and that is the wall, which gives character and defines the place of the column (Figure 23). Although separated from the wall, the column is still bound to the form; direction is initiated by the wall. Mies reveals in this arrangement a complex picture of play between opposites. Its ambiguity is presented in the dining area of the Tugendhat House. The position of the two columns next to the window is determined, on the one hand, by the necessity of structural order and, on the other, by the trace of the wall. The columns stand on the perimeter of a hypothetical circle realized by the extension of the curved wall.

Moreover, the House for a Bachelor reveals the ultimate rift between the load-bearing function of the wall and its abstract representation. The free expressive character of the

Figure 23. Mies van der Rohe, Tugendhat House, Brno, 1928–30, plan of ground floor. Photograph courtesy of Mies van der Rohe Archive, the Museum of Modern Art, New York. Gift of the architect.

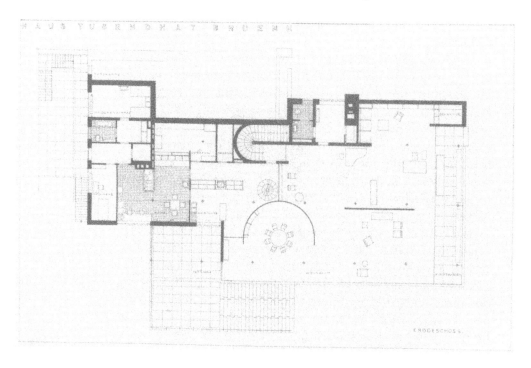

74

wall in conjunction with the presence of the column is a successful simulation of the Brick Country House. Yet the exchange of the partition for the wall disrupts the conventional image of a structural order. The dining area of the House for a Bachelor serves as a difficult vantage point from which to read the structural system: on one side, we have the two chromium columns standing in front of a wall; on the opposite, a partition's solid extension rises up to the ceiling and obstructs the columns behind it, prompting a false reading of the wall as a structural element.

Nevertheless, these projects share the following two interrelated points. First, the elementarist juxtaposition of their architectonic elements recalls the De Stijl compositions. Yet beyond the formalistic content of the latter, the elementarist character of the wall, column, slab, and podium of the Pavilion deconstructs the metaphysics of the inside and outside relationship (Figure 24). Second, the continuous distillation of symbolic and representational content from the architectural object legitimizes the very process of abstraction. As a result of the design strategies, the wall and column acquire new meanings. In Miesian language, the wall is reduced to

Figure 24. Mies van der Rohe, Barcelona Pavilion, 1928. Photograph courtesy of Mies van der Rohe Archive, the Museum of Modern Art, New York.

the facticity of its material. For instance, Mies's treatment of
marble does not correspond to any denotative meaning that
the material might have obtained in the history of modern
architecture.[18] Losing its ontological connection with earth,
the wall in Mies's architecture represents "the empty
wall . . . the pure wall" or "the silent wall" (citing Wassily
Kandinsky as the last word in a chain of attributions).[19] The
column, on the other hand, beyond its verticality, neither refers to nature and the human body nor recalls any stylistic
metaphor. Instead, it has been pulled into a self-indulgent
process of abstraction. In Mies's design, the cross shape and
the other formal configurations of the column represent one
choice among many compositional possibilities initiated by
the shapes of steel products. However, this set of design pol-
icies ends in dispensing with the metaphysical context of the
tectonic of column and wall. The resultant void houses an architectural discourse in which Mies designated construction
as the ultimate criterion of "truth."

Truth and construction return us to the theme that most
concerned Mies: the relationship between technology and
culture of dwelling. By opening the domain of cultural signification to that of technology, Mies formalized the architectural language of steel and glass. But his incorporation of
modern technology into the culture of dwelling has more
significant implications than either the analogies Le Corbusier would make between architecture and machine or the
Bauhaus's programmatic intention to reconcile art with technology. According to Francesco Dal Co, "It is the architecture of Mies and not the steel constructions of the Bauhaus
which tells of the withering of modern experience."[20] Yes,
Mies was aware of this metamorphosis. The limits of his
architecture are drawn skillfully within the dilemma of modern artistic production – that is, the liquidation of the language of art by technique.[21] Simply put, how could one
utilize technology without entitling architecture to the nihilism of technology? And more important, by what critical
means could one save the constructed world from the ever-
expanding domain of cultural commodification? In regard to
these questions, the Farnsworth House and the 50 × 50
House are exemplary; they represent the beginning of an end.
These two designs convincingly suggest that the realization
of Mies' speechless art of construction demanded the elimi-
nation of the wall and the presence of the column as governing tectonic element.

The 50 × 50 House is Mies's homage to the avant-garde desire to transform our perceptual experiences through technology (Figure 25). To this end, the dislocation of the column from the corner to the middle of the enclosing glass planes challenges the expected correspondence between form and structure. This disjunction is a shocking statement. Meanwhile, the plan exploits the notion of the open plan to the extent that its void represents the loss of memory and intimacy. Finally, the transparent silence of its skin recalls Malevich's *White on White* painting. One wonders if Mies was not pushing the dialectic of enclosure and openness to the limit. Drawing on Synthetic Cubism, he attempted to bridge the gap between an object and its representation. The glass partition of the 50 × 50 House metaphorically carries enclosure to its functional limits. By pushing the columns to the outside of the skin of the house, Mies releases enclosure from any structural or stylistic function. His glass plates are impenetrable enclosures. The sheer dialogue between openness and enclosure illustrates the critical quality of silence and the dialectic of solitude and waiting in Mies's work. The illuminated space faces us in silence. Its muteness speaks to us through the gentle and contingent setting of the house on its site. The same "indifferent" touch connects its columns to the roof and the earth. Indifferent to place as well as to humanity's presence on the earth and under the sky – as Martin Heidegger would have sought – Mies's work discloses the

Figure 25. 50 × 50 House project, 1950–1. Hedrich Blessing photograph, courtesy of the Chicago Historical Society.

impossibility of dwelling. One can argue that, parallel to the avant-garde, Mies closes the circle of negation, abstraction, and construction.

Now, what would have been the next design stage beyond such speechless constructs? Is there any devaluation of tradition left to accomplish? Or is there any formal territory yet to be emancipated from its representational burden? The answer to these questions is reflected in the idea of object type, a structural construct whose repeatability is an act of resistance to the tradition of the new. In Mies's later work, including the Bacardi Office Building, the Crown Hall, and, finally, the New National Gallery, each demonstrates a sense of returning from his early thoughts. One might argue that Mies had come to have second thoughts about the nihilistic dimension of technology and, therefore, the essential need for a spiritual order in cultural reproduction.[22] However, Mies's primary concern is still the space, technology, and their translation into a building art whose thematic was rooted in the unresolved problems of nineteenth-century architectural discourse. One can pursue Gottfried Semper's tectonic of the earthwork and the framework, already present in the Barcelona Pavilion, in most of Mies's later architecture. Yet Mies's resistance to the tradition of the new and his emphasis on the demythification of construction disclose the formative themes of a minor language of architecture.[23] That language deterritorialized the hegemonic power of the modern architecture and in return subjected Mies's work to the same process of reification that other cultural products were already entitled to. This paradox speaks for the consequences of the ultimate infiltration of modern technology into architecture. The simple and yet austere character of the curtain wall of the Seagram Building and the details connecting steel columns to the masonry wall at the corners of the buildings of the Illinois Institute of Technology campus lost their author's signature very soon: they were devoured by the building industry and became "readymades," details at the service of commercial architecture (Figure 26).

What conclusions should one draw from this reading of Mies? Did he reduce architecture to the level of a "thing," or commodity, or does his work speak for the end of the idea of resistance against a social system whose culture is at the verge of total commodification? These are important questions having to do with a critical analysis of the state of postfunctionalist architecture. I would like, however, to emphasize, one more time, the potentiality of the idea of montage for

Figure 26. Mies van der Rohe, Illinois Institute of Technology campus, Chicago, 1942, detail. Photograph courtesy of the author.

radicalizing the process of demythification of construction from the point where it is possible to find traces of montage, not only in Mies's various collage drawings, but in the Pavilion as well. The fragmented character of the vertical and horizontal planes, as well as the ways in which these elements relate to each other, emulate a spatial experience that could be associated with two aspects of montage. First, the absence of any spatial hierarchy in this building evinces a spatial organization whose enclaves are not mere fragments or traces of a preconceived entity. Rather, each is experienced as a self-contained spatial construct. Second, these independent enclosures relate to each other in a way that defies the conventional part–whole relationship. Somewhat similar to the plot of a film, each spatial enclave of the Pavilion is and yet isn't part of a whole perceivable in its totality. The space one experiences in the Pavilion recalls Piranesi's engraving, in which the threshold between inside and outside is blurred and the metaphysics of holistic vision of architectural totality is shaken. I contend that montage provides a critical mode of thinking and making whose implications for post-Miesian architecture is more far-reaching than the postmodernist simulation of historical forms.

CHAPTER 6

CONSTRUCTION OF THE NOT YET CONSTRUED

. . . it is reasonable to know yourself, and not to search into what the ancients have made if the moderns can make it.[1]

This statement by Giovanni Battista Piranesi captures the quintessence of what Charles Baudelaire characterizes as *la modernité*.[2] Baudelaire's discourse on modernity abrogates the indisputable superiority of antiquity. Underestimating the values of the so-called golden ages, he attempts to "apprehend the specific nature of the present state of human affairs."[3] From this point of view, the notion of modernity, understood in comparison to its past, is replaced by what Michel Foucault frames as the "ontology of the present."[4] Piranesi's journey to Rome and his etchings suggest that his architectural discourse transcends the thematic structure of the quarrel between the ancients and the moderns.

Yet the most articulated studies on the current state of architecture remain in the discursive canon of the quarrel between the ancients and the moderns. Alberto Pérez-Gómez locates the origin of the continuing critical situation of Western architecture in the late eighteenth century. Accordingly, he stands in sympathy with a historical past in which "the primacy of perception as the ultimate evidence of knowledge was never questioned."[5] Likewise, Joseph Rykwert, in identifying "the first moderns" in the architecture of J. L. N. Durand and Claude Perrault, depicts a nonproblematic state of architectural discourse in which the harmonious interaction of hearing and seeing constitutes its normative dimension.[6] These readings of history demonstrate a theoretical attempt that aims at overcoming historicist relativism. However, by isolating certain aspects of architectural tradition, these views "encompass the totality of an epoch as its sense or fundamental structure."[7] This approach not only perpetuates a perception of history that is not transient; it widens the already existing gap between tradition and the present architectural practice. There is more to learn from Louis Kahn, who, wondering how he was contemplating the present, came to grasp "the new" in the "mythical archaic."

In the current theater of cultural affairs, the debate between the ancients and the moderns is revitalized. The void opened up by the culture industry stages a challenge before the entire field of modern architecture. The classical forms and their attributed universal values are conceived as tradition. Once more, we are facing a subtle confrontation between the past and a utopia of the future with regard to technological achievements. In this connection, I agree with Vittorio Gregotti that we should "refer instead, as a central theme of architecture, to the truth of the present."[8] In response, I will attempt to unfold aspects of the ontology of architecture today by focusing on the two themes of architecture's origin and its construction.

The cover picture of Marc-Antoine Laugier's book *An Essay on Architecture* illustrates the problematic of architectural representation (Figure 27). The main compositional element of this picture is a figure of a female who leans on the remnants of a classical column. Her hand directs a genie's attention to a structure set in nature. By presenting two interrelated readings of this picture, I would like to address the question of the origin of architecture and its relation to construction.

This composition illustrates the biological relationship between female and child, symbolizing the prolific essence of nature. It also refers to the pedagogical dimension of parenthood: analogically, it posits Laugier as a learned man who has the capacity to shed light on architectural matters. The structure, however, contains the major elements of a shelter. Four tree trunks uphold a pediment-like roof whose leaves and branches cover the space defined by the posts and protect anyone in the enclosure from discomfort. The plainness of the structure points to the rational depths of architecture. "It is by approaching the simplicity of this model," maintains Laugier, "that fundamental mistakes are avoided."[9]

However, in regard to my inquiry, I find Neil Levine's reading suggestive. He believes that Laugier's hut affirms the "ultimate aim of representation in architecture, which is the establishment of a continuity between figure and ground,"[10] that is, between a building and its setting. Levine stops short of elaborating this anthropological understanding of architecture beyond its representational dimension.

Figure 27. Marc-Antoine
Laugier, Cover page for
Essai sur l'architecture (Paris,
1755). From the Resource
Collection of the Getty
Center for the History of
Art and the Humanities,
Santa Monica, California.

At another level, the figure of the female is the point of
departure. Her attachment to the classical column connotes
the conventional perception of the female as the guardian of
tradition. Viewed in the historicality of Laugier's discourse,
tradition here refers to the idea of the classical.[11] The mes-
sage of the picture goes beyond the question of the origin of
architecture. It unfolds the relationship between building
and architecture.[12] Representation is expressed by the distance between the position of the seated woman and the hut.
Her gaze is the medium through which a simple hut is "pic-

tured" as the basic structure of architectonic composition.
Classical architecture is represented as a result of a projection
carried out by human faculty. Yet the compass and ruler
held in the left hand of the figure offer the proper design
means of guaranteeing a rational simplicity against the
whimsical tendencies of Baroque architecture. This reading
suggests that Laugier's discourse fulfills the two major vectors of the tradition of Western epistemology – rationalization of means–end relationship and projection. One might
claim that theories of architecture have not gone beyond this
representational interpretation of classical architecture since
the Renaissance.

Pérez–Gómez argues for the existence of a certain level of
rational conceptualization in Vitruvius's discourse.[13] Here I
would like to present another reading of Vitruvius that discloses a different view of the issue of the origin of architecture and its relation to construction. Implicit in Laugier's
argument is the presence of three constructive components of
existence: nature, humankind, and architecture. Nevertheless, Laugier conceives of these three elements in the context
of representation, through which the poetic dimension of the
distance between the gaze and the thing is obscured.

Vitruvius presents a particular condition with regard to
the constructive elements. In describing the origin of fire, he
proposes a notion of *techne* in which dwelling, in the Heideg-
gerian sense, is implied; thinking and making take place in
association with the human body and the specific place.
Here, the constructive aspects of architecture are presented as
part of a larger and more fundamental perception of construction, that is, production (preparation of fire), the act of
gathering, and finally the process of communication.[14] It is
the feeling of warmth experienced through the sense of
touch, the intimacy of the body in relation to the fire, and the
achieved comfort that culminates in the desire for settlement
and the act of dwelling. A room is made for space, cleared
within a boundary and freed from its setting.[15] Through this
process, one comes to terms with nature and achieves an understanding of the body. "We ourselves are after all buildings
which have to stand on little feet and must not fall. What do
we do in order not to fall?" Paul Klee responds, "We stand
erect and rooted in the earth."[16] Therefore, one might argue
that the place of the human body in architecture is not merely
confined to its proportional reflection on architectonic elements; but the act of construction and discovery of the body

and its tactile sensibilities are critical aspects of the process of dwelling.

We may conclude that Vitruvius's later reflections on wooden construction as the origin of the Greek temple differ from Laugier's speculation that the hut is the basic structure of architecture. Wolfgang Herrmann correctly terms this phenomenon in Vitruvian discourse as the "theory of trans-formation."[17] His argument recalls Gottfried Semper's consideration of timber construction and its significance for monumental buildings. However, for Semper, the wooden hut was not the material model for the temple.[18] As an ethnological object, the Caribbean hut exhibited in the Crystal Palace called Semper's attention to the logical connections between practical arts and their impact on architecture. There are two points in Semper's historical observation: at one level lies the formal and thematic sharing between different productive activities. For example, the idea of hangings and hedges in separating and forming a space preceded stone and wooden wall constructions. The same thing is clear from Semper's historical findings on the transposition of timber motifs into the iron- and metalwork of Etruscan candel-abras.[19] In a similar vein, one might suggest that the formal plasticity of the base of a classical column narrates the ossified feeling of a moment when a syrup-like material touches a hard surface. In this sense, the classical column was neither a representative nor an imitative entity, but it was an analogy to load-bearing needs and what Semper terms *Stoffwechel* – that is, "the carrying over of motives visually from one material to another."[20] Implicit in Semper's discourse was the ontological dimension of "the transposition among different activities." At this level, the intercommunication between various works of art instituted a chain of constructive syntaxes that defined the material condition of existence. For Semper, the hearth, the terrace, the roof, and the wall were not formal categories. These four elements of a dwelling embodied some moments of life as they were experienced through the four arts of ceramics, masonry, joinery, and textiles.

Semper's discourse on the origin of architecture discarded both historicism and the idea of epochal perfection. Construction and construing architecture in association with other elements of everyday life took place within a discursive canon in which the ontology of the present was its point of departure. "How to change old forms, consecrated by necessity and tradition, according to our new means of fabrication" became Semper's motto on tectonic and type. By focusing on these two themes, Semper revealed an associative reading of architecture in which building is a fragment of a larger totality, that is, the construction of the condition of life. It is both the concrete results of other constructive works and their images printed in memory that conjugates the obscurity of meaning and the complexity of architecture.

As I pointed out in my opening statement, Piranesi holds a critical position in this rupture. Certain of his etchings depict the ontological relationship between body, nature, and architecture.[21] Associating these three elements with the concrete condition of human life, Piranesi integrated the finite nature of the body and the power of knowledge with the architecture of ruin and punishment.

Human existence and its living conditions unfold an architectural discourse of which construction is the formative theme. Here construction should neither imply composition, as it was perceived by Renaissance architects,[22] nor be reduced and narrowed down to the exigencies of the production line. Along with these interpretations, we see the constructs of De Stijl, for which the product displays the mere technique of fabrication. The Schroder-Schrader House and Gerrit Rietveld's red-blue chair exemplify abstract plastic construction. Now, drawing from Vitruvius's discourse, I believe that there is the possibility of framing the notion of construction in terms of associative dialogue among production, place, and architecture.[23]

Construction is the act of locating an architectural thing in the vastness of our living conditions. To erect a wall is to make a room for shadow in the infinite lightness of a place. After all, "a wall is a wall," and it stands there between earth and sky in relation to humankind. Was not Kahn attempting to associate architecture with the metaphoric domain of the purification of the body of water when he explained the stone ledges placed in the brick wall of the art gallery at Yale University as an architectonic means that, on a rainy day, would allow the water "to wash the wall at intervals"?[24] One thinks of the poetics of built-form and its relation to the "tactile resilience" of the place-form and the "sensorium of the body." I also think of Kenneth Frampton's thought on an Islamic court, where "the ambulatory experience of the place-form is inseparable from the sound of the water with which it invariably resonates" or "by the intensity of light or darkness, heat and cold, or by the aroma of material, or by the almost palpable presence of enclosure or by the body's own momentum."[25] These observations sustain an architectural discourse whose major themes and notions are not derived from formal and aesthetic abstractions; instead, this discourse refers to the domain of existence that contains the cultural dynamics of our present condition of life.

In conclusion, I would like to return to Gregotti's argument. From his point of view, the architectural work "is not a compulsory reference to the need for provisions which is traditionally connected to the idea of project, as much as to the constitution of a special vantage corner from where it is possible to illuminate some points of the present condition."[26] This position implicitly addresses the question of the ontology of the present and its construing. To understand the present project of architecture, it might not be necessary to assign a set of values as a claim of truth against the ongoing ones. By contrast, the ontology of the present rests in the gaps and contradictions that sustain our postmodern architectural discourse. Among these, the failure of the project of the historical avant-garde and an essential change in technology might be identified as the two vectors of postmodern conditions. While the first development brings to an end the idea of the grand narrative, or "project," the latter makes it almost impossible to think of the cultural apart from the technical.[27] In other words, the vanguard position of the artistic production of the early twentieth century is shaken by current mass-media technology. Ironically, the change in technology recycles what was already the pride of Cubism, Surrealism, and Dadaism. In this paradox, the position of postmodern and deconstructivist architecture seems naive, mainly because of their "modernist" war against the near past, if not also for their constructs, which assess nothing more than reactivating the thematics of modern artistic discourses. Yet one should stress the fact that we have come far enough from the anxieties that would have found their spatial comfort in Adolf Loos's interiors, from the historical atmosphere in which Le Corbusier desired to tune up with the *Zeitgeist,* or from Mies van der Rohe, whose work might best be conceived as a joint standing midway between tradition and civilization. This distance and its sociocultural conditions have been nullified by the very process of secularization of the context of the life-world, to use Husslerian terminology, to the point that one's participation in different spheres of social life, and the multiplicity of values generated,

has shattered the space through which one could develop a
self-centered ego.[28]

Furthermore, it should be stressed that secularization has
created a temporal situation that can plausibly be called a beginning. According to Martin Heidegger, a beginning "contains the undisclosed abundance of the unfamiliar and
extraordinary, which means that it also contains strife with
the familiar and ordinary."[29] We are at the threshold of dis-
covering different sensational layers of the body; we are finding out that the "truth" content of language is fiction, and
we are confronting a mode of production that pretends that
the nonreal is real. More important, we are experiencing a
sense of simultaneity that questions the distance between here
and there, unfolding a spatiality that is not confined by visible boundaries. If this is a plausible reading of present conditions, then I would suggest that the demythification of
construction means the recollection – a countermemory that
"distorts,"[30] – of Semper's discourse on the tectonic. One
example might be a tectonic figuration in which the simultaneity of structure and ornament is stressed to the point that
architecture turns into an ornament. One might, in Semper
pursue a belief in the separation between ornament and structure. However, his emphasis on the "artifice" as the true
character of art and, more important, his characterization of
the tectonic of the Assyrian column suggest that, for Semper,
dressing is an artistic means of dematerializing form until
a distinction between the structural and the ornamental
becomes impossible. This recalls Hans-Georg Gadamer's
discussion that architecture "not only embraces all the decorative aspects of the shaping of space, including ornament,
but is itself decorative in nature."[31] I would add that what is
by nature decorative in architecture is the tectonic of a space
making, in which the "strong" distinction between what is
essential to construction, and what as ornament is an excess,
is weakened. The natural state of simultaneity between structure and ornament comes from the Greek word *Kosmos,* signifying both "universe" (order?) and "decoration." This
analogy becomes important when one reads in Semper that,
somewhat similar to dance and music, architecture is a cosmic art. Music and dance differ from the imitative arts in that
a distinction between what is essential to them and what is
excessive is almost impossible. This line of consideration is
also suggestive of a different understanding of the symbolic
dimension of architecture. Traditionally, the symbolic function of architecture was an attribute of its monumentality,

signifying by its classical language a definitive universality and the everlasting perception of these values in humanist discourse. And yet, "emptied" of its representational connotations, a monument is an ornament par excellence, the significance of which does not rest in the fixation of a set of values, but in pointing to the occurrence of an event that forms a background for our collective experience (Semper's artifice?), generating a multiplicity of interpretation. Vitruvius speaks of event in a narrative through which he makes a distinction between the Corinthian column and the Doric and Ionic ones. The latter two characterize the gender aspect of the relationship between the body and building, while at the same time each alludes to a province and its customs, respectively. The Corinthian, in contrast, recalls the event of the death of a maiden and its aftermath. According to Vitruvius, Callimachus, a sculptor, saw the remnants of the goblets put in a basket during the funeral of the young girl and fixed the proportions of the Corinthian column accordingly.[32] Semper emphasized the "theatricality" of the afterlife of an event by suggesting that "the monuments were scaffolding intended to bring together" not only various cultural artifacts, but "the crowds of people, priests, and the processions."[33] It is outside the objectives of my argument here to discuss the idea of "theatricality." However, I would like to stress the point that the tectonic of "theatricality" differs from the scenographics of postmodernism and the arbitrary formal playfulness of deconstructivist architecture – both disclosing the postfunctionalist theoretical inclination to see architecture as a sign or a text. Yet stage sets have always been considered a theatrical presentation of the life-world. A reversal of this representational paradox might suggest a Semperian follow-up to the tectonic figuration of the Russian Constructivist set designs. Nevertheless, following Vattimo, I would argue that this stage of symbolism is attainable only through the secularization of the metaphysical context of the tectonic. These lines also suggest the ways in which such a tectonic figuration would disclose the simultaneity of inside–outside spaces, in which an opening becomes a window opening into the world. That window motif, indeed, unfolds the multiplicity of enclosure and exposure by translating into architecture other spatial experiences of the same kind that are taking place in different spheres of cultural activity.[34] This multiplicity, the exchange of themes from one ensemble to another, also speaks for the idea of montage.

The demythification of construction accommodates the tectonic to the existing subjective and objective conditions of life, making room for wonder and imagination.[35] In Kahn's work at Dhaka, one confronts forms that do not correspond with our immediate memories. These alien and yet known forms are cut, magnified, and joined together to maintain the secularization of construction. His tectonic, while it stresses the importance of grounding architecture in the earth, exhibits the world in two ways as it faces the sky: by fragmentation and dis-joint. This concept speaks for our present perceptual experience and in a tectonic figuration that discloses the structural-symbolic of a concrete frame embedded in a masonry enclosure. There is nothing nostalgic or futuristic in this line of thinking. Rather, it underlines the perception that the surviving structure of architecture is not to be kept in coded form or in technology per se. Rather, it will survive in recollection of the tradition of an architectural theory at work in the realist architecture of the turn of the century, and its continuation, although in a "distorted" form, in Loos's architecture. Obviously, I am not advocating any esteem for historicism. Why should one think of the myth of particular historical experiences or, for that matter, the myth of the deconstruction of demythification in a purview of the nihilism of technology that constantly checkmates every proposed grand narrative? Nor am I advocating the death of architecture wrapped in different sorts of Hegelian prophesies of the end of art. There is no point in thinking of architecture outside the domain of life-world, through which the thematics of architectural discourse are coded and recoded in line with the prevailing technostatic and cultural transformation. Otherwise, how would one characterize how the articulations of the seam connecting the building to the earth expressed in the Rennaisance rustication of the base, and recoded in the Miesian tectonic of the earthwork and the framework, differ from that of Corbusian *piloti?*

NOTES

1. MONTAGE: RECODING THE TECTONIC

1. According to Hannah Arendt, "The actual work of fabrication is performed under the guidance of a model in accordance with which the object is constructed. This model can be an image beheld by the eye of the mind or a blueprint in which the image has already found a tentative materialization through work. In either case, what guides the work of fabrication is outside the fabricator and precedes the actual work process in much the same way as the urgencies of the life process within the laborer precede the actual labor process." See Arendt, *The Human Condition* (Chicago: University of Chicago Press, 1974), p. 140.

2. Argan continues, "Architectural elements such as columns, capitals, cornices, and so on, could now be constructed outside the shop and then put in place according to the architect's design, just as prefabricated elements are used today." Giulio Argan, *The Renaissance City* (New York: Braziller, 1969), p. 14.

3. This is a topical theme in architectural discourse. The subject has been elaborated from different points of view. Alberto Pérez-Gómez argues that positivism as the source of modern consciousness initiated an architectural understanding that has no interest in the transcendental dimensions of meaning in architecture. Yet for Manfredo Tafuri, the modernist reaction against classicism is not an arbitrary choice, but an aspect of Western thought that has opened up since the Renaissance. See Pérez-Gómez, *Architecture and the Crisis of Modern Science* (Cambridge, Mass.: MIT Press, 1983), and Manfredo Tafuri, *Theories and History of Architecture*, trans. Georgio Verrecchia (New York: Harper & Row, 1980).

4. Vitruvius, *De Architectura*, trans. Morris Morgan (New York: Dover, 1960), p. 5.

5. On this last point see George Hersey, *The Lost Meaning of Classical Architecture* (Cambridge, Mass.: MIT Press, 1988). For the mimetic dimension of classicism, see Demetri Porphyrios, "Classicism Is Not a Style," *Architectural Design* 52, nos. 5–6 (1982), pp. 51–7.

6. Leon Battista Alberti, *On the Art of Building in the Ten Books*, trans. Susan Edria Bassnett (New York: Braziller, 1969), p. 7.

7. Ibid.

8. Jean Baudrillard, *Simulations* (New York: Semiotext(e), 1983), p. 87.

9. Alberti, *On the Art of Building*, p. 156.

10. Elaine Scarry, *The Body in Pain* (New York: Oxford University Press, 1985), pp. 161–80.

11. I am alluding to a book with the same title by Marshall Berman, *All That Is Solid Melts into Air: The Experience of Modernity* (New York: Penguin, 1988).

12. Scarry, *The Body in Pain*, p. 244.

13. G. L. Hersey, *Pythagorian Palaces* (Ithaca, N.Y.: Cornell University Press, 1976), p. 117.

14. While defining architecture in terms of the Vitruvian trinity, Andrea Palladio relegated the first part of his book to "universal rules" covering the preparation of materials and the ways they might be put to use from foundation to roof. See Andrea Palladio, *The Four Books of Architecture*, trans. M. Morgan Hickey (New York: Dover, 1960), p. 5.

15. Ibid., p. 26.

16. Arendt, *The Human Condition*, p. 301.

17. Vitruvius, *De Architectura*, p. 155.

18. Ibid., p. 41.

19. Agnes Heller, *Renaissance Man*, trans. Richard E. Alle (Boston: Routledge & Kegan Paul, 1978), p. 395.

20. Michel Foucault, *The Order of Things* (New York: Vintage, 1973), p. 29.

21. Palladio, *Four Books of Architecture*, p. 27.

22. Ibid., p. 31.

23. Ibid., p. 11.

24. For elaboration on this theme, see my concluding remarks in this chapter.

25. Arendt, *The Human Condition*. Arendt argues that the first "tentative glances into the universe through an instrument, at once adjusted to human senses and destined to uncover what definitely and forever must lie beyond them, set the stage for an entirely new world and determined the course of other events, which with much greater stir were to usher in the modern age" (p. 257).

26. Paolo Rossi, *Philosophy, Technology and the Arts in the Early Modern Era*, trans. Salvator Attanasio (New York: Harper Torch Books, 1970), p. 142.

27. Arendt, *The Human Condition*, p. 296.

28. Joseph Rykwert, "Positive and Arbitrary," in *The First Moderns* (Cambridge, Mass.: MIT Press, 1980), pp. 23–53.

29. Hans-Georg Gadamer, *The Relevance of the Beautiful* (Cambridge University Press, 1986), pp. 13–20.

30. Sergio Villari, *J. N. L. Durand* (New York: Rizzoli, 1990), p. 57. Villari relates Durand's analytics to the scientific thoughts explored by Condillac and sees in Durand's *Leçons d'architecture* a text comparable to our present structuralist discourse on general grammar and the principle of arbitrariness.

31. See Galileo's proposition on the relationship between proportion and the strength of structural elements. Galilei Galileo, *Dialogues Concerning Two New Sciences*, trans. H. Crew and A. de Salvio (New York: Dover, 1954), p. 130.

32. Alexander Tzonis, *Aspects of Mechanization in Design: The Rise, Evolution and Impact of Mechanics in Architecture*, Publication Series in Architecture (Cambridge, Mass.: Harvard University, Graduate School of Design, 1980). A revised and expanded version of this piece was published as "The Mechanization of Architecture and the Birth of Functionalism," *VIA*, no. 7 (1984), pp. 121–44.

33. Marc-Antoine Laugier, *An Essay on Architecture*, trans. Wolfgang Herrmann and Anni Herrmann (Los Angeles: Ingalls, 1977).

34. According to Herrmann, "Differing from all previous writers, [Laugier] interpreted the classical principle of the balanced interplay of the whole and its parts in a concrete sense by demanding that the actual construction of a building should be formed by the members hitherto regarded as decoration." See Wolfgang Herrmann, *Laugier and Eighteenth Century French Theory* (London: Zwemmer, 1962), p. 21. Also important for my discussion on the tectonic is the distinction Herrmann notices between Laugier's normative discourse on the origin of architecture and Semper's.

35. Laugier, *Essay on Architecture*, p. 71.

36. Foucault, *The Order of Things*, p. 218.

37. J. N. L. Durand quoted in Sergio Villari, *J. N. L. Durand*, p. 64.

38. Louis-Etienne Boullée, "Architecture: Essay on Art," in Helen Rosenau, ed., *Boullée and Visionary Architecture* (New York: Harmony, 1976), p. 89. Anthony Vidler understands this aspect of Boullée's architecture to be a major step away from classical wisdom. According to Vidler, independent of its classical "garment," the traditional "sense of a building that embodied beauty in its proportions and in its three-dimensional geometries was gradually subordinated to the idea of a geometrical order that followed the dictates of social or environmental needs." See Vidler, *The Writing on the Wall* (Princeton, N.J.: Princeton Architectural Press, 1987), p. 3.

39. Sergio Villari also makes an analogy between the blank upper section of David's painting and the unadorned walls in Boullée's and Claude-Nicolas Ledoux's work as well. See Villari, *J. N. L. Durand*, p. 13.

40. Italo Calvino, *Six Memos for the Next Millennium* (Cambridge, Mass.: Harvard University Press, 1988), p. 23.

41. Antony Vidler, "Notes on the Sublime: From Neo-classicism to Postmodernism," *Canon*, 3 (1988), p. 172.

42. Joseph Rykwert, "Inheritance or Tradition?" *Architectural Design Profile*, 49, nos. 5–6 (1979), pp. 2–6.

43. Hubert Damisch, "The Space Between: A Structuralist Approach to the Dictionary," *Architectural Design Profile*, nos. 3–4 (1980), pp. 84–9.

44. Ibid.

45. Quoted in translation in Wolfgang Hermann, *In What Style Should We Build?* (Santa Monica, Calif.: Getty Center for Publication, 1992), p. 151.

46. Eugène-Emmanuel Viollet-le-Duc, *The Architectural Theory of Viollet-le-Duc*, ed. M. F. Hearn (Cambridge, Mass.: MIT Press, 1990), p. 86. Also see Viollet-le-Duc, "Lecture VII," *Lectures on Architecture* (New York: Dover, 1987), vol. 1, p. 270.

47. Kenneth Frampton, "Auguste Perret," in *Studies in Tectonic Culture* (Cambridge, Mass.: MIT Press, forthcoming).

48. John Ruskin, *The Stones of Venice* (New York: Da Capo, 1960). Ruskin argues that "the special condition of true ornament is, that it be beautiful in its place, and nowhere else, and that it aid the effect of every portion of the building over which it has influence; that it does not, by its richness, make other parts bald, . . . and it is fitted for its service by what would be fault and deficiencies if it had no special duty" (p. 113).

49. Eugène-Emmanuel Viollet-le-Duc, "General Observations on the External and Internal Ornamentation of Buildings," in *Lectures on Architecture* (New York: Dover, 1987), pp. 171–246, at 177.

50. Thus, Ruskin continues, "I suppose, no one would call the laws architectural which determine the height of a breastwork or the position of a bastion. But if to the stone facing of that bastion be added an unnecessary feature, as a cable moulding, *that* is Architecture." John Ruskin, *Seven Lamps of Architecture* (New York: Farrar, Straus, & Giroux, 1981), pp. 15–16.

51. Viollet-le-Duc, "General Observations," p. 200.

52. Quoted in Roger Scruton, *The Aesthetics of Architecture* (Princeton, N.J.: Princeton University Press, 1979), p. 174.

53. Eugène-Emmanuel Viollet-le-Duc, "Style: The Manifestation of an Ideal Based on a Principle," in *The Foundations of Architecture* (New York: Braziller, 1990), pp. 231–63.

54. I am using the ideas of "the death of subject" and "simulation" as defined by Michel Foucault and Jean Baudrillard, respectively. Fredric Jameson considers these two themes to be critical for an understanding of the postmodern discourse. To question the role of author does not mean its literary "death" or the banishment of meaning in art. The idea of the death of the subject opens a space for the post-avant-garde era, through which the meaning of a work is embedded neither in the work itself nor in the symbolic-formal intentions of the artist. Rather, the work attains its meaning from the lived experience of a given cultural space. The death of the author could also be seen as an inevitable discursive development of the crisis of the grand narrative, i.e., utopia. In conjunction with the promotion of electronic technology, the concept of the death of the author endorses Walter Benjamin's assertion of the impossibility of experience in the era of mechanical reproduction. Baudrillard pushes this line of thinking to its extreme: "Reality no longer has the time to take on the appearance of reality. It no longer even surpasses fiction." Baudrillard, *Simulations*, p. 154. On the death of the author, see Michel Foucault, *Language, Counter-memory, Practice* (Ithaca, N.Y.: Cornell University Press, 1972). For Jameson, see "Periodizing the 60's," in Sohnya Sayres and Andres Stephanson, eds., *The 60's Without Apology* (Minneapolis: University of Minnesota Press, 1984), pp. 178–209.

55. Kenneth Frampton, "Rappel à l'Ordre: The Case for the Tectonic," *Architectural Design Profile*, no. 84 (1990), pp. 19–25.

56. Harry Francis Mallgrave reminds us that "the problems that industrialization and speculation (capitalism) have brought to art, Semper feels, are quite serious and deeply rooted; the proliferation of new materials, methods, and machinery have flooded the marketplace with products and means that designers have had little time to contemplate, let alone master. This devaluation of the idea and of labor has led, in turn, to a devaluation of meaning, so that traditional art

produced by hand comes to be seen as eccentric." See Semper, *The Four Elements of Architecture and Other Writings*, trans. Harry Francis Mallgrave and Wolfgang Herrmann (Cambridge University Press, 1989), p. 28. Implied in Mallgrave's last point, the devaluation of idea and value, is the idea of secularization, the automization of the spheres of value and experience.

57. Walter Benjamin, "The Storyteller," in *Illuminations*, trans. H. Zohn (New York: Schocken, 1969), pp. 83–110.

58. Ibid., p. 84. On this subject also see Richard Wollin, "Benjamin's Materialist Theory of Experience," in *Walter Benjamin: An Aesthetic of Redemption* (New York: Columbia University Press, 1982), pp. 213–49, especially the part in which Wollin associates Benjamin's ideas on the shock experience with Freud's belief that confronting the modern life, consciousness becomes more protective than registering the outside stimulus.

59. Semper, *The Four Elements*, p. 146.

60. Ibid., p. 144. Speaking of the different ways that Otto Wagner and Semper saw the future of architecture in an industrial age, Harry Francis Mallgrave argues that Semper overestimated the potentialities of his time and "failed to foresee that capitalism, with its new speculative modes of production, would tend to promote rather than reject historical values and forms." See Mallgrave's introduction to Otto Wagner, *Modern Architecture* (Santa Monica, Calif.: Getty Center for the History of Art and the Humanities, 1988), p. 13.

61. Susan Buck-Morss reminds us of the importance of the concept of "wish image" for Benjamin. According to Benjamin, the nineteenth century could not afford to utilize the new technology without connecting it with primordial forms. Semper, in his criticism of materialists, argues that "at the risk of falling into the same error that I criticize [antiquarianism], I see myself forced to go back to the primitive conditions (*Urzusände*) of human society in order to come to that which I actually propose to set forth." Semper, *The Four Elements*, p. 102. On Benjamin, see Susan Buck-Morss, "Mythic Nature: Wish Image," in *The Dialectics of Seeing* (Cambridge, Mass.: MIT Press, 1989), pp. 110–58.

62. Semper, *The Four Elements*, p. 104.

63. Ibid.

64. Ibid., p. 124.

65. For a translation of Adolf Loos's article, see "The Principle of Cladding," in *Spoken into the Void* (Cambridge, Mass.: MIT Press, 1982), pp. 66–9. And for Mark Wigley, see "Architecture After Philosophy: And the Emperor's New Paint," *Journal of Philosophy and the Visual Arts* (1990), pp. 84–95. One can read Wigley in line with Loos's distinction between structure and the covering, as well as his belief that "the architect's general task is to provide a warm and livable space. He decides for this reason to spread out one carpet on the floor and to hang up four to form the four walls. But you cannot build a house out of carpets. Both the carpet on the floor and the tapestry on the wall require a structural frame to hold them in the correct place. To invent this frame is the architect's second task" (Loos, *Spoken into the Void*, p. 66).

66. Semper, *The Four Elements*, p. 126.

67. Ibid., p. 23.

68. Carl Botticher, "The Principles of Hellenic and Germanic Ways of Building," in Hermann, trans., *In What Style Should We Build?* pp. 147–67, at 158.

69. Ibid., p. 154.

70. Ibid., p. 163.

71. Wolfgang Herrmann, *Gottfried Semper in Search of Architecture* (Cambridge, Mass.: MIT Press, 1984), p. 151.

72. Semper, *The Four Elements*, p. 249.

73. Ibid., p. 252.

74. Marco Frascari, "The Tell-the-Tale Detail," *VIA*, no. 7 (1984), pp. 23–37.

75. Heinrich Hubsch, quoted in Herrmann, *In What Style Should We Build?* p. 72.

76. This triad is defined and extensively discussed by Henri Lefebre in *The Production of Space* (Cambridge: Blackwell, 1991), p. 38. It is out of the purview of this piece to discuss Lefebre's insightful text. However, I would like to mention two related texts that are important for my argument. The first is Walter Benjamin's "The Work of Art in the Age of Mechanical Reproduction," in which he suggests that "the mode of human sense perception changes with humanity's entire mode of existence." Our sense perception has drastically changed with the separation of artifact from its aura. The second is Gilles Deleuze and Félix Guattari, *A Thousand Plateaus*, in which they define and map the differences between what Deleuze calls smooth and striated space in an analogy to felt and fabric and the spatial connotation stimulated by the production process of these two textile industries. See Benjamin, *Illuminations*, pp. 217–52, and Deleuze and Guattari, *A Thousand Plateaus* (Minneapolis: University of Minnesota Press, 1987), pp. 474–500.

77. Deleuze and Guattari, *A Thousand Plateaus*.

78. According to Edward Said, "If a filial relationship was held together by natural blood and natural forms of authority, the new affiliative relationship changes these bonds into what seems to be transpersonal forms – such as guild consciousness, consensus, collegiality, professional respect, class, and hegemony of a dominant culture. The filliative scheme belongs to the realm of nature and of "life," whereas affiliation belongs exclusively to culture and society." See Said, *The Words, the Text, and the Critic* (Cambridge, Mass.: Harvard University Press, 1983), p. 20.

79. I am borrowing the term "distanciation" and its implications for my concluding remarks from Paul Ricoeur's discourse "Speaking and Writing," in *Interpretation Theory: Discourse and the Surplus of Meaning* (Fort Worth: Texas Christian University Press, 1976), pp. 25–44.

80. Romano Luperini, "Symbol and Allegory: From Goethe to Luckacs, from Marx to Benjamin," *Differentia*, no. 5 (Spring 1991), p. 101.

81. Ibid.

82. See Gianni Vattimo, "The End of (Hi)story," *Chicago Review*, 35, no. 4 (1986), pp. 20–30. See also Vattimo, *The End of Modernity* (Baltimore: Johns Hopkins University Press, 1988), especially the last chapter. For my reading of Vattimo, see "A Monument to the End of Modernity: Implications of Gianni Vattimo's Discourse on Architecture," in Marc M. Angelil, ed., *On Architecture, the City, and Technology* (Stoneham: Butterworth-Heinemann, 1990), pp. 77–9.

2. ARCHITECTURE AND THE QUESTION OF TECHNOLOGY: TWO POSITIONS AND THE "OTHER"

A shorter version of this essay "Poetics of Technology and the New Objectivity," was published in *Journal of Architectural Education*, 40, no. 1 (Fall 1986), pp. 14–19.

1. Eugène-Emmanuel Viollet-le-Duc, "Architecture in the Nineteenth Century – Importance of Method," *Discourses on Architecture*, trans. B. Bucknall (New York: Grove, 1959), pp. 447–87.

2. William Morris, "The Revival of Architecture," in N. Pevsner, ed., *Some Architectural Writers of the Nineteenth Century* (Oxford University Press, 1972), pp. 269–324.

3. Viollet-le-Duc, "Architecture in the Nineteenth Century," p. 446.

4. Morris asserts: "History taught us the evolution of architecture. It is now teaching us the evolution of society; and it is clear to us and even to many who refuse to acknowledge it, that the society which is developing out of ours will not need or endure mechanical drudgery." He adds that the new society "will produce to live, and live to produce, as we do." His revolutionary optimism drew him to postulate that, "under such conditions, architecture . . . will again become possible." "Revival of Architecture," pp. 269 and 324.

5. For a summary of this school of thought, see Benedetto Gravagnuolo, *Adolf Loos: Theory and Works*, trans. C. H. Evans (New York: Rizzoli, 1982).

6. Adolf Loos, *Spoken into the Void*, trans. Jane O. Newman (Cambridge, Mass.: MIT Press, 1982), pp. 104–6.

7. Nikolaus Pevsner, *Pioneers of Modern Design* (New York: Penguin, 1975).

8. Walter Gropius, "Gropius at Twenty-Six," *Architectural Review* 130 (July 1961), pp. 49–51.

9. Matei Calinescu, *Faces of Modernity: Avant-Garde, Decadence, Kitsch* (Bloomington: Indiana University Press, 1977), pp. 101–2.

10. Walter Gropius, *Scope of Total Architecture* (New York: Collier, 1974), pp. 19–29. Implied in Gropius's statement is the core of a view of secularization that considers the formative themes of the modern world evolving out of a metamorphosis of *the* Christian kingdom. In fact, Gropius's desire "to form a new guild of craftsmen" is a case in point and should be distinguished from the Gothic revivalists.

11. Walter Gropius, "Programme of the Staatliche Bauhaus in Weimar," in Hans M. Wigler, ed., *The Bauhaus* (Cambridge, Mass.: MIT Press, 1978), pp. 31–3.

12. Adorno, quoted in Gravagnuolo, *Adolf Loos*, p. 60.

13. Marcel Franciscono, *Walter Gropius and the Creation of the Bauhaus in Weimar* (Chicago: University of Illinois Press, 1971), p. 24.

14. Walter Gropius, *The New Architecture and the Bauhaus* (Cambridge, Mass.: MIT Press, 1976), p. 54.

15. Walter Benjamin, "The Work of Art in the Age of Mechanical Reproduction," in *Illuminations*, trans. H. Zohn (New York: Schocken, 1969), pp. 217–52.

16. Gropius, *Scope of Total Architecture*, p. 69.

17. Heinrich Wolfflin, *Principles of Art History*, trans. M. D. Hottinger (New York: Dover, 1950).

18. Viollet-le-duc, *Discourses on Architecture*, p. 44.

19. Incidentally, in 1891, on the occasion of the publication of his *Sketches, Projects and Executed Buildings* (trans. Edward Vance Humphery [New York: Rizolli, 1987], p. 18), Otto Wagner spoke favorably for the triumph of realism in art and suggested a balanced approach to the artistic and utilitarian demands of architecture. For the implication of realism in German architecture, I am indebted to Harry Francis Mallgrave and his trustful submission of the following three unpublished essays on this subject and *Sachlichkeit* (originally from the Otto Wagner Symposium, Nov. 3–5, 1988, at the Getty Center for the History of Art and the Humanities). For a reading of Otto Wagner in this context, see J. Duncan Berry, "From Historicism to Architectural Realism: On Wagner's Source," and Harry Francis Mallgrave, "From Realism to Sachlichkeit: Otto Wagner and the Polemics of Modernity in the 1890." For the entertainment of *Sachlichkeit* within realist architecture and the transformation of the term into *Neue Sachlichkeit,* see Stanford Anderson, "*Sachlichkeit* and Modernity, or Realist Architecture."

20. Walter Gropius, "The Theory and Organization of the Bauhaus," in Tim Benton, Charlotte Benton, and Dennis Sharp, eds., *Architecture and Design, 1890–1939* (New York: Watson-Guptill, 1975), pp. 119–27, at 125.

21. Fritz Schmalenbach, "The Term *Neue Sachlichkeit,*" Art Bulletin 22, no. 3 (1940), pp. 161–5.

22. Ibid.

23. Francisco, *Walter Gropius,* p. 28. The idea of *Sachlichkeit* has its roots in that circle of German realist architecture that, drawing on Otto Wagner's reading of Semper's tectonic, perceived new techniques and materials as a means to recode the practicality, comfort, and hygiene of English domestic architecture, while emulating the vernacular content of William Morris's thoughts. According to Harry Francis Mallgrave, the word *Sachlichkeit* was introduced to architectural discourse by Richard Streiter, and later Muthesius reinterpreted it in the context of duality between norm and style. See Mallgrave, 19. On the role of Hermann Muthesius in introducing the English style to Germany, see Pevsner, *Pioneers of Modern Design,* pp. 30–9.

24. Noticing Muthesius's nationalistic tendencies, Stanford Anderson associates him with Richard Streiter and the latter's emphasis on a regional content of *Sachlichkeit,* securing a position for Muthesius within German realist architecture. I would suggest that, from the outset, one should differentiate William Morris's interest in regionalism as a source of resistance from the secularization of dwelling, a process whose intensification was the goal of Muthesius's sociopolitical project. For Anderson, see note 19.

25. Francisco, *Walter Gropius,* p. 31.

26. Gropius continues: "Whenever man imagines he has found eternal beauty he falls back into imitation and stagnation. True tradition is the result of constant growth; its quality must be dynamic, not static, to serve as an inexhaustible stimulus to man." See Walter Gropius, *Scope of Total Architecture* (New York: Collier, 1974), p. 67.

27. Gropius, "The Theory and Organization of the Bauhaus," p. 147.

28. Peter Eisenman, "Aspects of Modernism: Maison Domino and the Self-Referential Sign," *Oppositions*, nos. 15–16 (Winter–Spring 1979), pp. 119–29.

29. Le Corbusier, *Towards a New Architecture*, trans. F. Etchells (New York: Praeger, 1960).

30. Stanislaus von Moos, *Le Corbusier: Elements of Synthesis* (Cambridge, Mass.: MIT Press, 1979).

31. Baudelaire, quoted in Calinescu, *Faces of Modernity*, p. 57.

32. For Le Corbusier, the Parthenon is a machine par excellence. To him, the formal configuration of the Parthenon neither represents nor alludes to anything; the parts and elements relate to each other as the parts of a machine would do. Thus, the significance of the Parthenon, as with every object of beauty, is its "composition," which stimulates the spectator's eyes. Here, Le Corbusier presents the Kantian view of "aestheticism," which looks at art in relation to feeling.

33. On the question of painting in modern architecture see John Summerson, "Architecture, Painting and Le Corbusier," in *Heavenly Mansions* (New York: Norton Library, 1963), pp. 177–94. Also see Colin Rowe and Robert Slutzky, "Transparency: Literal and Phenomenal," in *The Mathematics of the Ideal Villa and Other Essays* (Cambridge, Mass.: MIT Press, 1984), pp. 159–83.

34. Le Corbusier, *Towards a New Architecture*, p. 11.

35. Le Corbusier, quoted in F. Katherine Fischer, "A Nature Morte," *Oppositions*, nos. 15–16 (Winter–Spring 1979), pp. 157–65.

36. At the beginning of the twentieth century, the idea of abstraction was dominant in art and artistic creativity. In line with the historical debate on the relationships between nature and civilization, the modernist conception of life was so remote from nature that it became the abstract. Banham Reyner, *Theory and Design in the First Machine Age* (New York: Praeger, 1967), p. 150. Also see Paul Valéry's account on the importance of abstraction in works of art, in *Collected Works*, ed. J. Matheius (Princeton, N.J.: Princeton University Press 1972), vol. 8, p. 46.

37. Allan Janik and Stephen Toulmin, *Wittgenstein's Vienna* (New York: Touchstone, 1973), p. 99.

38. Adolf Loos, "Architecture," in Benton, Benton, and Sharp, eds., *Architecture and Design*, pp. 41–5.

39. Adolf Loos, "Cultural Degeneracy," in Benton, Benton, and Sharp, eds., *Architecture and Design*, pp. 40–1, at 40.

40. Hans Poelzig, "The Architect," in Benton, Benton, and Sharp, eds., *Architecture and Design*, pp. 56–60.

41. Giorgio Grassi argues that Poelzig and Tessenow were two architects who emphasized métier. This statement becomes more significant when we compare Tessenow's views of the differences between technique and art. See Grassi, "On the Question of Decoration," *Architectural Design Profile*, 54, nos. 5–6 (1984), p. 33.

42. Loos, "Architecture," p. 45.

43. Poelzig, "The Architect," p. 60.

44. Martin Heidegger, "The Question Concerning Technology," *Basic Writings*, ed. D. F. Krell (New York: Harper & Row, 1977), pp. 287–322. One might argue that Heidegger's interpretation of *techne* consciously avoids the "loss of the aura" in favor of a discussion of the

essence of technology. The implication of this is to map the relationship between architecture and technology beyond the scope of instrumental conception of technology.

45. Heidegger defines "knowing" as "the primordial and permanent seeing out behind that which is merely there . . . knowing as the ability of putting into work of being as, in each case, a definite being." For further elaboration, see John Loscerbo, *Being and Technology* (Boston: Martinus Nijhoff, 1981), p. 22.

46. Heidegger, "The Question Concerning Technology," p. 293.

47. Giulio Argan argues that the type "is formed through a process of reducing a complex of formal variants to a common root form." The latter, he continues, "has to be understood as the interior structure of a form or as a principle which contains the possibility of infinite formal variation and further structural modification of the type itself." See Argan, "On the Typology of Architecture," *Architectural Design*, 33, no. 12 (1963), p. 565. For a thorough survey of the debate on typology, see Micha Bandini, "Typology as a Form of Convention," *AA Files*, no. 6 (1986), pp. 72–82; Rafael Moneo, "On Typology," *Oppositions*, 13 (Summer 1978), pp. 23–45. On the place of type in modern architecture, see Anthony Vidler, "The Third Typology," in *Rational Architecture* (Brussels: Archives d'Architecture Moderne, 1978), pp. 28–32.

48. Loos, "Architecture," p. 45.

3. ADOLF LOOS: THE AWAKENING MOMENTS OF TRADITION IN MODERN ARCHITECTURE

1. Walter Benjamin, "Paris, Capital of the Nineteenth Century," in *Reflections* (New York: Harcourt Brace Jovanovich, 1978), p. 148.

2. Quoted in Susan Buck-Morss, *The Dialectics of Seeing: Walter Benjamin and the Arcade Project* (Cambridge, Mass.: MIT Press, 1989), p. 67.

3. For Loos, "tradition is no more the enemy of development than the mother is an enemy of the child. Tradition is a reservoir of strength from countless generations, and the firm foundation for a healthy future." Quoted in Stanford Anderson, "The Legacy of German Neoclassicism and Biedermeir: Behrens, Tessenow, Loos, and Mies," *Assemblage*, no. 15 (1991), pp. 63–87. Exploring the relation of modern German architects to the architecture of the eighteenth century, Anderson characterizes Loos's approach to the historical past in the following words: "Loos's understanding of tradition acknowledges conflict, inconsistencies, and contradictions within the cultural setting, and consequently, the need to act critically, to criticize the operative conventions, embracing what I have termed a critical conventionalism" (p. 77).

4. According to Fritz Neumeyer, in Berlin, "the train would cut right through a museum complex and run next to a wall covered on the other side with Greek and Egyptian sculptures." And he continues, "Like knives they fragmented the classical architectural composition by isolating forms and disassembling the hierarchical canon with its progressive horizontal layers of *rutica, piano nobile*, etc." See Neumeyer, "The Second-Hand City: Modern Technology and Changing

Urban Identity," in Marc M. Angelil, ed., *On Architecture, the City, and Technology* (Stoneham, Mass.: Butterworth-Heinemann, 1990), pp. 16–25, at 17.

5. Joseph Rykwert, "Positive and Arbitrary," in *The First Moderns* (Cambridge, Mass.: MIT Press, 1980), pp. 23–53. Exploring different facets of the debate, Rykwert underlines its significance for "the nature of history and the relation of the past to thinking, to speculation" (p. 25).

6. Walter Benjamin, *Illuminations*, trans. H. Zohn (New York: Schocken, 1969), p. 257.

7. "Only a very small part of architecture belongs to art: the tomb and the monument. Everything else, everything which serves a purpose, should be excluded from the realm of art." And in an indirect reference to the Werkbund, he continues, "But the fusion of art with craft has caused both them and all mankind untold damages." Adolf Loos, "Architecture," in Tim Benton, Charlotte Benton, and Dennis Sharp, eds., *Architecture and Design, 1890–1939* (New York: Watson-Guptill, 1975), pp. 41–45, at 45.

8. Benedetto Gravagnuolo, *Adolf Loos: Theory and Works*, trans. C. H. Evans (New York: Rizzoli, 1988). Also see David Leatherbarrow, "Interpretation and Abstraction in the Architecture of Adolf Loos," *Journal of Architectural Education*, 40, no. 4 (1987), pp. 2–9.

9. According to Demetri Porphyrios, the metaphoric operation of material should be understood in a twofold manner: "It is a metaphor that alludes to the associative value springing on the one hand from the very nature of materials *qua* matter, and on the other from the particular technique with which they have been treated." See Porphyrios, *Sources of Modern Eclecticism* (London: Academy Editions, 1982), p. 50.

10. Gravagnuolo, *Adolf Loos*, pp. 125–33.

11. Ibid., p. 51.

12. Adolf Loos, "Interiors in the Rotunda," in *Spoken into the Void*, trans. Jane O. Newman (Cambridge, Mass.: MIT Press, 1982), p. 24. Here, one might suggest the similarities between Loos's understanding of a house and Benjamin's notion of the "aura," referring to a historical juncture at which an object is identified with a broad network of social and historical processes. According to Benjamin, the aura . . . withers away through technical reproduction. See Benjamin, *Illuminations*, p. 221.

13. According to Benjamin, "The uniqueness of a work of art is inseparable from its being embedded in the fabric of tradition." And he continues: "The unique value of the authentic work of art has its basis in ritual, the location of its original use value." See Walter Benjamin, "The Work of Art in the Age of Mechanical Reproduction," in *Illuminations*, pp. 217–52 at 223. Here, Benjamin is primarily concerned with the impact of mechanization on art and its reception by the mass. However, implied in his concluding remarks is the idea that mechanization, while undermining the aura, might stimulate a state of distraction that not only is important for the optical aspect of art, but can also form "habits" endemic for collective reception of architecture; for "the tasks which face the human apparatus of perception at the turning points of history cannot be solved by optical means, that is, by contemplation, alone. They are mastered gradually by

habit under the guidance of tactile appropriation" (p. 240). This last point is significant if read in conjunction with Benjamin's claim that the tactility developed out of habits plays a determinant role in the ways buildings are appropriated.

14. Loos, "Interiors in the Rotunda," p. 24.

15. Quoted in Kurt H. Wolf, *The Sociology of George Simmel* (New York: Free Press, 1964), p. 422.

16. Keaton argues that during his visit to the United States, Loos had seen some interiors of Richardson's houses, in particular the Glessner House in Chicago. L. K. Keaton, *American Architecture Comes of Age* (Cambridge, Mass.: MIT Press, 1972), p. 114. Speaking of H. H. Richardson's influence on the Steiner House, Gravagnuolo points out that "more than the details (such as the open brickwork and rafters, the lights hung from the ceiling, the rough look to the design of the furniture), it is the architectonic concept of the spatial continuum that attests to the refined evocation of the house of the American Pioneers." See Gravagnuolo, *Adolf Loos*, p. 139.

17. Loos, "The Principle of Cladding," *Spoken into the Void*, p. 67. I am using "dressing" for *Bekleidung*, as suggested in Harry F. Mallgrave, "Adolf Loos and the Ornament of Sentiment," *Midgard* 1, no. 1 (1987), pp. 79–87.

18. A distinction between "dress," and "dressing" is explicit in Loos's belief that "wood may be painted any color except one – the color of wood." Loos, "The Principle of Cladding," p. 67.

19. This statement is important to an understanding of secularization and its consequences for Gianni Vattimo's discourse on "weak thought" architecture. See Vattimo, "Myth and the Fate of Secularization," *Res,* no. 9 (1985), pp. 29–35.

20. Loos, "Architecture," p. 45.

21. Kenneth Frampton, *Modern Architecture: A Critical History* (New York: Oxford University Press, 1980), p. 44.

22. Stanislaus von Moos, "Le Corbusier and Loos," *Assemblage,* no. 4 (1987), pp. 25–37. Also see von Moos, *Raumplan Versus Plan Libre,* ed. Max Risselada (New York: Rizzoli, 1988).

23. Kenneth Frampton, *Modern Architecture,* p. 85.

24. Gianni Vattimo, "Dialectics, Difference, and Weak Thought," *Graduate Faculty Philosophy Journal* 10, no. 1 (1984), pp. 151–64. See also Vattimo, *The End of Modernity* (Baltimore: Johns Hopkins University Press, 1988).

4. MÉTIER: FRANK LLOYD WRIGHT'S TRADITION OF DWELLING

This chapter is a revised version of "Métier: The Tradition of Dwelling," *Traditional Dwelling* 16 (1989), pp. 1–22.

1. Frank Lloyd Wright, *In the Cause of Architecture,* ed. F. Gutheim (New York: Architectural Record Books, 1975), p. 123.

2. Walter Benjamin, "The Work of Art in the Age of Mechanical Reproduction," in *Illuminations* (New York: Schocken, 1969), pp. 217–52.

3. T. S. Eliot, "Tradition and the Individual Talent," in *Selected Prose of T. S. Eliot,* ed. Frank Kermode (New York: Harcourt Brace Jovanovich, 1965), pp. 37–44, at 38.

4. Adolf Loos, "Architecture," in Tim Benton, Charlotte Benton, and Dennis Sharp, eds., *Architecture and Design 1890–1939* (New York: Watson-Guptill, 1975), pp. 41–5.

5. Gottfried Semper, "London Lecture of November 11, 1853," edited by Harry F. Mallgrave, *Res 6* (Autuman 1983), pp. 5–31, at 12.

6. S. N. Kelly, *Frank Lloyd Wright: A Study in Architectural Content* (New York: Watkins Glen American Life Foundation, 1977).

7. I have in mind Richard Streiter and his articulation of realist architecture in terms of the demands of atmosphere or milieu. Although his ideas are rooted in the Arts and Crafts movement, as Stanford Anderson demonstrates, they attain a peculiar dimension in Adolf Loos. Anderson, "Sachlichkeit and Modernity, or Realist Architecture," from an unpublished manuscript; see chapter 2, note 19, this volume.

8. Henry Russell Hitchcock and Philip Johnson, *The International Style* (New York: Norton Library, 1966), p. 27. For a critical review of the exhibition, see Terence Riley, *The International Style: Exhibition 15 and the Modern Museum of Art* (New York: Rizzoli, 1992).

9. Walter Benjamin, "The Destructive Character," in *Reflections* (New York: Harcourt Brace Jovanovich, 1978), p. 302.

10. Terry Eagelton, *Walter Benjamin, or Towards a Revolutionary Criticism* (London: Verso, 1985), p. 59.

11. Frank Lloyd Wright and B. Brownell, *Architecture and Modern Life* (New York: Harper & Brothers, 1937), p. 17.

12. Against utopia, heterotopia unfolds a discursive formation that is disturbing because it undermines the ordering logic of language and destroys "syntax in advance, . . . but also that less apparent syntax with which causes words and things (next to and opposite one another) to hold together." Michel Foucault, *The Order of Things* (New York: Vintage, 1973), p. xviii. Also see Foucault, "Of Other Spaces," *Diacritics*, 16, no. 1 (Spring 1986), pp. 22–7.

13. Kelly, *Frank Lloyd Wright*, p. 53.

14. Le Corbusier, *Towards a New Architecture*, trans. F. Etchells (New York: Praeger, 1960), p. 68.

15. Mericia Eliade, quoted in Kelly, *Frank Lloyd Wright*, p. 169.

16. Frank Lloyd Wright, *The Living City* (New York: Meridian, 1958), pp. 19–25. Also see Vincent Scully, *Frank Lloyd Wright* (New York: Braziller, 1985), p. 21.

17. Wright, and Brownell, *Architecture and Modern Life*, p. 25.

18. Frank Lloyd Wright, *The Future of Architecture* (New York: Horizon, 1953), p. 200.

19. Quoted in "Three Works by F. L. Wright and Other Writings," *Zodiac*, no. 17 (1967), pp. 11–46.

20. Wright, *The Living City*, p. 154.

21. For a detailed analysis of this facade and its association with Viollet-le-Duc's thought, see Edward E. Ford, *The Details of Modern Architecture* (Cambridge, Mass.: MIT Press, 1990), pp. 169–77.

22. Wright, *The Future of Architecture*, p. 107.

23. Adolf Loos, "The Principle of Cladding," in *Spoken into the Void* (Cambridge, Mass.: MIT Press, 1982), pp. 66–9.

24. Vincent Scully compares the vertical and horizontal stripes of this facade with the abstract paintings of Piet Mondrian. This analogy stops short of analyzing architectonic expressions as a result of a dialogical

relationships between the idea of dressing and the tectonic. See Scully, *Frank Lloyd Wright*.

25. Frank Lloyd Wright, *An Autobiography* (New York: Horizon, 1977), p. 170.

26. Manfredo Tafuri and Francesco Dal Co, *Modern Architecture* (New York: Abrams, 1979), p. 159.

27. Philip D. Verner, "Wisdom of Barbarism," in *Vico's Science of Imagination* (Ithaca, N.Y.: Cornell University Press, 1982), pp. 193–221.

28. On the concept of abstraction in Wright's architecture, see Neil Levine, "Abstraction and Representation in Modern Architecture: The International Style of Frank Lloyd Wright," in *AA Files*, no. 11 (Spring 1986), pp. 3–21.

29. Again, one should stress the regional content of Wright's architecture since it would become a backdrop for Lewis Mumford's presentation of regionalism as an alternative to the Beaux Arts' historicism and the functionalism of the international style. I am referring to Mumford's lecture at the occasion of a seminar held by the Museum of Modern Art, titled "What Is Happening to Modern Architecture?" See *Museum of Modern Art Bulletin* (Spring 1948), pp. 4–21. Also see Mumford, "Skyline," *New Yorker* (Oct. 11, 1947), pp. 104–8. The 1950s were important for the future development of American art and architecture. Along with the aforementioned concern for the future of architecture, there was also an intellectual debate at work, aiming to purge the artistic avant-garde of its political content. This eventually ended in the realization of American abstract painting. See Serge Guilbaut, *How New York Stole the Idea of Modern Art* (Chicago: University of Chicago Press, 1983). Interestingly, one can pursue the implications of Guilbaut's observations for architecture almost half a century later in MOMA's exhibition of deconstructivist architecture.

30. Sibly Moholy-Nagy, "F. L. W. and the Aging Modern Architecture," *Progressive Architecture* 40, no. 5 (1959), p. 137.

5. MIES VAN DER ROHE: THE GENEALOGY OF COLUMN AND WALL

This chapter is a revised version of an article published in *Journal of Architectural Education*, 42, no. 2 (1989), pp. 33–6.

1. See note 23.

2. Colin Rowe, *The Mathematics of the Ideal Villa and Other Essays* (Cambridge, Mass.: MIT Press, 1982), p. 35.

3. For an interpretation of Mies's work in the guise of philosophical discourse, see P. Serenyi, "Spinoza, Hegel and Mies: The Meaning of the New National Gallery in Berlin," paper abstract, *Journal of the Society of Architectural Historians* 30 (Oct. 1971), p. 240. See also Franz Schulze, *Mies van der Rohe: A Critical Biography* (Chicago: University of Chicago Press, 1985), pp. 90–4, and Fritz Neumeyer, *The Artless Word* (Cambridge, Mass.: MIT Press, 1992). Neumeyer not only provides an in-depth analysis of Mies's concept of the "building art," but maps the vicissitudes of Mies's discourse in the context of contemporary intellectual and philosophical issues.

4. As Manfredo Tafuri has suggested, the most important aspect of avant-garde thought was the attempt to desecrate existing values in

order to open the path to a critical understanding of art and society. See Tafuri, *Architecture and Utopia*, trans. B. L. Penta (Cambridge, Mass.: MIT Press, 1977), p. 56. On the influence of the Suprematist painters in Mies, see Kenneth Frampton, "Mies van der Rohe and the Significance of Fact, 1921–23," in *Modern Architecture: A Critical History* (New York: Oxford University Press, 1980), pp. 161–6. For an analysis of the theme of renunciation in Mies, see K. Michael Hays, "Critical Architecture," *Perspecta* 21 (1984), pp. 14–24.

5. For the scope of Mies's relationships with different intellectual circles of his time, see Schulze, *Mies van der Rohe*, pp. 83–130.

6. Ibid., p. 35.

7. Ulrich Conrads, *Programs and Manifestos on Twentieth Century Architecture* (Cambridge, Mass.: MIT Press, 1975), p. 154.

8. Mies van der Rohe, "Aphorisms on Architecture and Form," quoted by Philip C. Johnson, *Mies van der Rohe* (New York: Museum of Modern Art, 1947), pp. 184.

9. Alfred Barr, *Cubism and Abstract Art* (New York: Museum of Modern Art, 1964), p. 156.

10. On the interrelationship between ornament and beauty, Alberti concludes: "Beauty is somewhat lovely which is proper and innate, and diffused over the whole body, and ornament somewhat added or fastened on, rather than proper and innate." See Leon Batista Alberti, *Ten Books on Architecture*, ed. Joseph Rykwert (London: Alec Tiranti, 1955), p. 113.

11. Ibid., p. 48.

12. Michel Foucault, *The Order of Things* (New York: Vintage, 1973), p. 29.

13. Alberti, *Ten Books on Architecture*, p. 14.

14. On this subject, see Joseph Rykwert, "Inheritance or Tradition?" *Architectural Design Profile* 49, nos. 5–6 (1979), pp. 2–6.

15. Alberti, *Ten Books on Architecture*, p. 48.

16. Hubert Damisch, "The Column and the Wall," *Architectural Design Profile* 49, nos. 5–6 (1979), pp. 18–25.

17. For the first view, see Wolf Tegethof, *Mies: The Villas and Country Houses* (New York: Museum of Modern Art, 1985), and for the second, see Schulze, *Mies van der Rohe*.

18. I refer the reader to Alvar Aalto's treatment of this material in Alajarvi Town Hall or Ekenas Savings Bank in Tammisaari, where, according to Demetri Porphyrios, the metaphoric operation is based not on marble's material facticity but on its "stylistic density," i.e., in "the encoded meanings that classicism had already assigned to it." See Porphyrios, *Sources of Modern Eclecticism* (London: Academy Edition, 1982), p. 50.

19. Quoted by L. Hilberseimer, *Contemporary Architecture: Its Roots and Trends* (Chicago: Theobald, 1964), p. 200.

20. Francesco Dal Co, *Figures of Architecture and Thought* (New York: Rizzoli, 1990).

21. Speaking of the vicissitudes of the relationship between art and technology, Theodor Adorno argues that "while technique is the epitome of the language of art, it also liquidates that language." See Adorno, *Aesthetic Theory* (New York: Routledge & Kegan Paul, 1984), p. 310. The same process of liquidation is at work in Mies. His architecture renounces any representational or subjective intentionality. Michael

Hays discusses this point and suggests that while Mies resisted the total absorption of subject in the "social subtext," it is Ludwig Hilberseimer whose forms absorb this subtext in its totality. See Hays, *Modernism and the Posthumanist Subject* (Cambridge, Mass.: MIT Press, 1992), p. 195.

22. Following Guardini's philosophy, Mies accepted technology "as a means of realization and also seeing it as a potential threat." For Guardini, this ambivalent approach to technology is the only way to sustain the vitality of life in the chaotic situation created by the project of modernity. See Fritz Neumeyer, *Artless Word*, especially chap. 6.

23. A minor language does not operate outside of an existing major one. Rather, it uses the major language's potentialities for purposes other than one would expect. According to Gilles Deleuze and Felix Guattari, such an act of problematization of language could result either in reterritorialization (James Joyce) or deterritorialization of a given hegemonic language (Kafka). See Deleuze and Guattari, *Kafka: Toward a Minor Literature* (Minneapolis: University of Minnesota Press, 1986), pp. 16–27. In line with this thinking, one could suggest that the multicentralities of Baroque architecture reterritorialized the Renaissance language and sustained the persistence of humanist values, whereas Piranesi's engravings deterritorialized the raison d'être of the classical language of architecture by shaking the coherent totality of those values.

6. CONSTRUCTION OF THE NOT YET CONSTRUED

1. Quoted in Johan Wilton-Ely, *The Mind and Art of Giovanni Battista Piranesi* (London: Thames & Hudson 1978), p. 78.

2. On Baudelaire's view of modernity, see Walter Benjamin, *Charles Baudelaire: A Lyric Poet in the Era of High Capitalism* (London: Verso, 1983). Also see note 3.

3. For the genealogy of the conception of modernity and its implications for the literary work of Baudleaire and Schlegal, see Tilo Schabert, "A Note on Modernity," *Political Theory* 7, no. 1 (1986), pp. 123–37.

4. Michel Foucault, "Kant on Enlightenment and Revolution," *Economy and Society* 15, no. 1 (1986), pp. 88–96. For Foucault, "modern" is conceivable in contrast to our prehistory and to what is still contemporary. According to John Rajchman, in Foucault's later writing, "modernity comes to refer to what in the past is still operative in our present." See Rajchman, *Michel Foucault: The Freedom of Philosophy* (New York: Columbia University Press, 1985), p. 31.

5. Alberto Pérez-Gómez, *Architecture and the Crisis of Modern Science* (Cambridge, Mass.: MIT Press, 1983). Before closing the final draft of this text, I had the chance to read Pérez-Gómez's introduction to the English translation of Claude Perrault's *Ordonnance*. Here, Pérez-Gómez folds the nihilism of present architectural theory into Perrault's discourse and correctly concludes that the latter "must be destructured, not simply nostalgically denied or falsely overcome." Therefore, Perrault's doubt about the attributed coherency between logos and mythos is not presented negatively, but rather is suggestive for a possible unfolding of a meaningful architecture. See Pérez-Gómez, "Introduction" to Claude Perrault, *Ordonnance for the Five*

Kinds of Columns After the Method of the Ancients (Santa Monica, Calif.: Getty Center for the History of Art and the Humanities, 1993), p. 38.

6. Joseph Rykwert, *The First Moderns: The Architects of the Eighteenth Century* (Cambridge, Mass.: MIT Press, 1980).

7. Theodor Adorno, "The Idea of Natural History," *Telos*, no. 60 (Summer 1984), pp. 111–24. Following Walter Benjamin's discourse on allegory, Adorno posits the notion of semblance, through which we can arrive at a dialectical understanding of convention: "If you sense an aspect of semblance in certain houses, then along with this semblance there is the thought of that-which-has-always-been and that it is only being recognized" (p. 124).

8. Vittorio Gregotti, "The Project of the Present," *Casabella* (Oct. 1986), pp. 2–3.

9. Marc-Antoine Laugier, *An Essay on Architecture*, trans. W. A. Herrmann (Los Angeles: Hennessey & Ingalls, 1977), p. 12.

10. Neil Levine, "Abstraction and Representation in Modern Architecture: The International Style of F. L. Wright," *AA Files*, no. 11 (Spring 1986), pp. 3–21.

11. In his approach to classical architecture, Laugier did not take a dogmatic attitude. Several times in his essay, he advocated change. However, he would not challenge the classical, which, according to Peter Eisenman, "evokes a timeless past, a golden age superior to the modern time or the present." See Eisenman, "The End of the Classical: The End of the Beginning, the End of the End," *Perspecta*, no. 21, (1984), pp. 154–173. For a sociological interpretation of the term "classical" and its formal system, see Alexander Tzonis and Liane Lefaivre, *Classical Architecture, the Poetics of Order* (Cambridge, Mass.: MIT Press, 1986).

12. On this subject, see Demetri Porphyrios, "Classicism Is Not a Style," *Architectural Design*, 52, nos. 5–6 (1982), pp. 51–7. Here, Porphyrios presents tectonic as the raison d'être of classical architecture. This position does not leave room for a tectonic discourse beyond the ontology of building initiated by classicism. In contrast, Gottfried Semper argues for the tectonic as a "cosmic art" whose ontology rests in the artistic experience and is attained through technical arts.

13. According to Vitruvius, "the meaning and beauty of architecture were dependent on rational order – the mathematical order of the cosmos as discerned in the motion of heavenly bodies and the proportions of the human body." Quoted by Alberto Pérez-Gómez, "The Myth of Daedalus," *AA Files*, no. 10 (1985), pp. 45–52. Pérez-Gómez does justice to Vitruvius when he discharges the possibility of any form of instrumental rationality before Descartes.

14. Vitruvius, *De Architectura*, trans. Frank Granger (Cambridge, Mass.: Harvard University Press, 1970), pp. 77–87. Joseph Rykwert points out the eclectic aspect of this passage and considers it the essential text for architects who are interested in the problem of the origin of architecture. According to him, Vitruvius's account "smacks of Stoic doctrine tinged by peripatetic empiricism." See Rykwert, "Reason and Grace," in *On Adam's House in Paradise* (Cambridge, Mass.: MIT Press, 1981), pp. 105–44.

15. Martin Heidegger, "Building Dwelling Thinking," in *Poetry, Language, Thought* (New York: Harper & Row, 1971), pp. 143–62. Heidegger speaks of the original "event," the event of lighting

(*Lichtung*) through which the community of nature disappears and things become nameable, intelligible to an understander. See Joseph P. Fell, *Heidegger and Sartre: An Essay on Being and Place* (New York: Columbia University Press, 1979), pp. 189–214.

16. Quoted in K. O. Werckmeister, "From Revolution to Exile," in Carolyn Lancher, ed., *Paul Klee* (New York: Museum of Modern Art, 1987), pp. 39–64. On the question of the human body and architecture, see Joseph Rykwert, "Inheritance or Tradition?" *Architectural Design* 49, nos. 5–6 (1979), pp. 2–6.

17. Wolfgang Herrmann, *Laugier and the Eighteenth Century French Theory* (London: Zwemmer, 1985).

18. On Semper's position on the hut, see Wolfgang Herrmann, *Gottfried Semper in Search of Architecture* (Cambridge, Mass.: MIT Press, 1984), pp. 165–73. On Semper's views on the origin of architecture, see Joseph Rykwert, "Necessity and Convention," *On Adam's House in Paradise* (Cambridge, Mass.: MIT Press, 1981), pp. 29–42. For a criticism of the conventional interpretation of Semper, see Rosemarie Haag Bleher, "On Martin Frohlich's Gottfried Semper," *Opposition*, no. 4 (Oct. 1974), pp. 146–53.

19. Gottfried Semper, "London Lecture," *Res* 6 (Autumn 1983), pp. 5–31.

20. Semper quoted in Harry Francis Mallgrave, "The Idea of Style: Gottfried Semper in London," Ph.D. dissertation, University of Pennsylvania, 1983, p. 302.

21. Marguerite Yourcenar presents the following picture of Piranesi's perception of body, nature, and architecture: "Even more often, instead of simply identifying the manmade shape with the human body, visual metaphor tends to reinstate the edifice within the ensemble of natural forces, of which our most complicated architectures are never anything but a partial and unconscious microcosm." (p. 100). Or: "The ruined temple is not merely a wreck on the sea forms; it itself is nature" (p. 101). See Yourcenar, *The Dark Brain of Piranesi and Other Essays*, trans. R. Howard (New York: Farrar Straus & Giroux, 1984), pp. 87–128.

22. Paolo Rossi, *Philosophy, Technology and the Arts in the Early Modern Era*, trans. Salvator Attanasio (New York: Harper Torch, 1970).

23. This dialogue becomes the maxim of what Kenneth Frampton encapsulates in "A Critical Theory of Building," *Modern Architecture and the Critical Present* (New York: St. Martin's, 1982), pp. 28–45.

24. Louis I. Kahn, quoted in John Cook and Heinrich Klotz, *Conversations with Architects* (New York: Praeger, 1973), pp. 178–218.

25. Kenneth Frampton, "Excerpts from a Fragmentary Polemics," *Art Forum*, no. 19 (Mar. 1981), pp. 52–8.

26. Gregotti, "Project of the Present," p. 3.

27. For a thorough discussion of these two points, see Gevork Hartoonian, "Avant-Garde: Re-Thinking Architecture," *Art Criticism* 7, no. 2 (1992), pp. 100–107.

28. The psychological aspects of this "closure" are discussed in Sigmund Freud's *Civilization and Its Discontent*. Theodor Adorno's discourse on the "culture industry" explores cultural implications of the same theme as the inevitable consequences of the project of the Enlightenment. The culture industry maps an administrative society such that the masses' relation to the work of art parallels their relation to con-

sumer goods. Also see Herbert Marcuse, *One-Dimensional Man* (New York: Bacon Press, 1964).

29. Heidegger, *Poetry, Language, Thought*, p. 76.

30. Between the two major tendencies of modernity – i.e., a regression into the historical past and the futuristic credo of "down with the past" – Gianni Vattimo's oeuvre in general, and his thoughts on *Verwindung* (recollection) in particular, are important for the present architecture. Reading Heidegger in light of Nietzsche, he argues that the ultimate destiny of secularization is recollection and distortion of the very content of the humanist history. See Vattimo, *The End of Modernity* (Baltimore: Johns Hopkins University Press, 1988). Also see Gevork Hartoonian, "A Monument to the End of Modernity: Implications of Gianni Vattimo's Discourse on Architecture," in Marc M. Angelil, ed., *On Architecture, the City, and Technology* (Stoneham: Butterworth-Heinemann, 1990), pp. 77–9.

31. For Gadamer, the decorative nature of architecture is embedded in its two-sided mediation: "to draw the attention of the viewer to itself, to satisfy his taste, and then to direct it away from itself to the greater whole of the context of life which it accompanies." See Hans-Georg Gadamer, *Truth and Method* (New York: Crossroad, 1985), p. 140. The major implication of the concept of the decorative is to think of architecture beyond the metaphysics of the "real work of art" or "the art of genius." My argument on monument/ornament reworks Gadamer's discourse from Gianni Vattimo's point of view. Gadamer's discussion of architecture as decorative remains within the vicissitudes of representational discourse. Vattimo, in contrast, accepts Walter Benjamin's characterization of the loss of the aura and conceives the attainability of the simultaneity of the "essential" and the "excessive" mainly by radicalizing the process of secularization. See Vattimo, "Ornament and Monument," *The End of Modernity*, pp. 79–89.

32. Vitruvius, *De Architectura*, book 4, p. 209. For the importance of ritual in classical architecture, see George Hersey, *The Lost Meaning of Classical Architecture* (Cambridge, Mass.: MIT Press, 1988). Following Gilles Deleuze, Ignasi de Sola-Morales Rubio discusses "a culture of event," through which one might produce an architecture that would undermine the permanence of metaphysics of inhabitation against the passage of time, i.e., the production of the place not "as the revelation of something existing permanently but as the production of an event." See Rubio, "Place: Permanence or Production," in Cynthia Davidson, ed., *Anywhere* (New York: Rizzoli, 1992), pp. 110–15. Rubio correctly speaks for the impossibility of following the classical canon for present-day architecture. However, his reading of Vitruvius is confined to the scope of academic convention and, in one way or another, justifies the current inclination of theories of architecture to draw their formative concepts from literary texts.

33. Gottfried Semper, *The Four Elements of Architecture and Other Writings*, trans. Harry Francis Mallgrave and Wolfgang Herrmann (Cambridge University Press, 1989), p. 65. Here, once more, Semper criticizes the point of view that conceives of architecture as an imitative art. Interestingly, a critique of theatricality is embedded in the realist content of Courbet's paintings that recurs for different purpose in both abstract painting and Malevich's architectural deliniations, where ge-

ometry is purified of any figurative element. Yet theatricality resurfaces in the kitsch character of much postmodern architecture. For the theme of theatricality in French realist painting of the early nineteenth century, see Michael Fried, *Courbet's Realism* (Chicago: University of Chicago Press, 1990). In Cubism's transition from analysis to synthesis, the focus of discussion was the concept of "construction" and its implication in late-nineteenth-century painting. The Parisian avant-gardes intended to depart from the "superficial realism of Courbet" in favor of Paul Cézanne, who combined the empiricism of senses with the conceptualization of the mind. For the concept of construction in the postwar development of French Cubism, see Kenneth E. Silver, *Esprit de Corps* (Princeton, N.J.: Princeton University Press, 1989), especially pp. 299–361. One might associate Semper's theatricality with what was alleged as Courbet's "superficial reality"; that is to say, the aspect that caused Courbet's realism to be perceived as superficial is what also makes tectonic "a structural-symbolic" expression of construction rather than the latter's "real" representation.

34. I use the word "translating" to suggest the impossibility of a one-to-one exchange between various cultural production activities and to restate the fact that throughout history the formative elements of architecture, i.e., ur-forms, are not changed. However, the concept of multiplicity, as presented here, would weaken the metaphysical context of humanist architecture.

35. I connect these two concepts because they resurface frequently in Louis Kahn's writings, and they were instrumental for architectural realism of the turn of the century. Architectural realism and Semper's association with it are discussed in James Duncan Berry, "*The Legacy of Gottried Semper: Studies in Spathistorismus,*" Ph.D. dissertation, Brown University, 1989. Interestingly enough, Fredric Jameson's analysis of the historicality of literary realism enables one to see a "life space in which the opposite and negative of such rationalization can be, at least imaginatively experienced" within the debris of the process of secularization. See Jameson, *The Political Unconscious* (Ithaca, N.Y.: Cornell University Press, 1981), p. 236.

INDEX

abstraction, 31, 70, 75–6, 78;
dominance of, 99n36; and "new
objectivity," 30

Adorno, Theodor, xii, 33, 105n21,
108n28

aestheticism, 3, 99n32

Alajärvi Town Hall, 105n18

Alberti, Leon Battista, 2, 8f, 9,
16, 50; aesthetic theory of, 72–3;
discourse on lineaments, 2, 7–8

Aalto, Alvar, 105n18

ancients and moderns, 44, 81–2

anthropological understanding of
architecture, xi–xii, 82

anti-formalism, 35

appearance, structure and, 7–8

arcades, 44

architect(s), 27, 32; Renaissance, 2,
7–8

architectonic composition, hut as
basic structure of, 84

architectonic elements, 40; in Alberti, 73; in Mies van der Rohe,
68, 69, 75; stair as, 53

architectural discourse, 3, 4, 29–
30, 40, 41, 90; break with classical thought in, 13–14; of
classicism, 5; Galileo's influence
on, 14; human existence in, 86–
7; of Le Corbusier, 38; of Mies
van der Rohe, 72; nineteenth-
century, 78; of Piranesi, 81;
themes of, 87; of Vitruvius, 84–
5, 86

architectural language, 36; autonomy of, 13; form in, 41; in Mies
van der Rohe, 68, 69;
nineteenth-century, 17–18; secu-

larization in, 69; of steel and
glass, 76; in Wright, 66, 67

architectural object (the): formal
understanding of, 34

architecture: abstract, 38; associative understanding of, 24–5; and
building, 18–19, 83–4; classification of, 3; commemorative role
of, xiii; as constructive component of existence, 84; design as
poetic expression of ideal, 2–3,
dialectics in history of, 17; as
discipline, 6–7; engineering separated from, 5; evolution of,
20–1; as expression, 15–16; hut
as basic structure of, 85; origin
of, 1, 82–4, 85–6; and question
of technology, 29–42; relation
with body and nature, 86; semantic autonomy of, 27; status
of, 6; temporal relationship with
its epoch, 30; as totality, 13; typological understanding of, 39;
unity of, 2

Arendt, Hannah, 10, 91n1

Argan, Giulio, 5

art: discourse of, 11; and machine,
37; realistic view of, 34; and
science, 29; and technique, 32;
and technology, 33–4, 36, 39,
43, 76, 105n21

art-form (*Kunstform*), 22, 23, 24,
27, 52; structural-spatial combinations, 25–6

"art of building," 37

artifacts, 3, 39, 56; authenticity of,
33, 48; technological development and, 35–6

INDEX

artifice, 88, 89
arts, high, 20
Arts and Crafts movement, xi,
    xiv, 9, 56, 57, 58
aura, loss of, 19, 33, 56, 57, 67,
    109n31; see also Benjamin Walter
autonomy: concept of, 13; seman-
    tic, 27
avant-garde, 104n4; in Mies van
    der Rohe, 77, 78; see also histori-
    cal avant-garde
avant-gardism, xiii, 68

Bacardi Office building, 78
Barcelona Pavilion, 72, 72f, 73,
    75, 75f, 78, 79–80
Baroque architecture, 14, 84,
    106n23
Barr, Alfred, 70
Baudelaire, Charles, 37, 81
Baudrillard, Jean, xii, 8, 94n54
Bauhaus school, 6, 30–1, 32, 33,
    43, 53, 76; new objectivity in,
    34–5; signet, 31, 31f
beauties, arbitrary and positive,
    14–15
beauty, 5, 35, 72; ornament and,
    9, 105n10; theoretical justifica-
    tion of, 13
Beaux Arts, 17
Beethoven, Ludwig van, 44
Behrens, Peter, 30, 35, 36, 57
being: and place, 58, 59
Bekleidung, xii, xiii, 52, 64; see
    also clothing; dressing
Benjamin, Walter, xii, 26, 28, 33,
    44–5, 48, 56, 94n54, 102n13,
    107n7; idea of "dialectical im-
    age," 43; loss of the aura,
    109n31; "Storyteller, The," 19;
    "wish image," 96n61; "Work of
    Art in the Age of Mechanical
    Reproduction, The," 96n76; see
    also aura, loss of
Blanc, Charles, 36–7
Bloch, Ernst, xv
body, 44, 84–5; analogy of archi-
    tecture and, 50; and/as building,
    50, 73, 89; relation with nature
    and arthitecture, 86–7; sensa-
    tional layers of, 88; and soul, 15;
    tactile and emotive dimensions
    of, 57

body–matter duality, 8–9
Bötticher, Karl, 17, 23, 25
Boullée, Etienne-Louis, 15, 16
Brick Country House, 70, 71f, 75
Brunelleschi, Filipo, 5, 7
Buck-Morss, Susan, 96n61
building: architecture and, 7, 18–
    19, 83–4; and/as body, 50, 73,
    89; design and, 16; empirical
    aspects of, 13; ornament in, 16;
    see also culture of building
building art, 69, 78
built-form, xii, xv; poetics of, 86
bürgerlich, 35

Calinescu, Matei, 32, 37
Calvino, Italo, 15
Condillac, Etienne B. de, 92n30
Caribbean hut, xi–xii, 85
Cartesian doubt, 5, 13
center, 59; loss of, 28
ceramics, 3, 20, 25–6, 85
Cézanne, Paul, 110n33
Chicago Tribune Building, 54–5
cinematography, 26
cities, 44; see also Metropolis
civilization: and culture, 52, 53;
    tradition and, 67, 87–8
classical (the), tradition as, 83
classical architecture, 40, 58, 84;
    tectonic as raison d'être of,
    107n12
classical discourse, 26; absence of
    concept of technology in, 29;
    break with, 14–16; concept of
    whole in, 27; in Mies van der
    Rohe, 68
classical language of architecture,
    6, 15, 29, 46, 64, 89, 106n23;
    break with, 36, 38; demise of, 2,
    19; figural character of, 37
classical thought: break with, 13–
    15; poetics of, 5–16; techne in,
    10–11; undermined by seculariz-
    ation, 12–13, 16
classical tradition: in Loos, 57;
    public architecture of, 46; in
    Wright, 58, 62, 64
classicism, 5, 58; modernist reac-
    tion against, 91n3
clothing, 7; see also Bekleidung;
    Semper, Gottfried
collage, 38

column(s), 6, 10–11, 13, 37, 38, 40, 50; classical, 54–5, 85; genealogy of, 68–80; Looshaus, 46; in Mies van der Rohe, 72–6; relation with beams, 14; in Renaissance, 11; *see also under specific type*
composition, 34, 86; significance in, 99n32
Concrete House, 70, 71f
construction, xii, 40, 78, 82–4, 85–6; concept of, 1–2, 9, 15; and construing, 24; demythification of, 68, 78, 79, 88, 90; design and, 2–3, 6; form and, 16–17; intention and, 27; organic understanding of, 26; and ornament, 16; and representation, 3; and signification, 16–28; as sole semantic dimension of architecture, 27; style and, 5, 6; theme of, 1–4; in theory of Mies van der Rohe, 69, 76, 77; and type, 10–11, 13
construction techniques, and logos of making, 13
Constructivism, 70
Coonly Playhouse, 61
core-form (*Kernform*), 22, 23, 52
cornice, 12, 62
Corps des Ponts et Chaussées, 5
cosmic art: architecture as, 3, 88; tectonic as, 107n12
costume, 24
crafts, craftspersons, 32, 33, 40; in German discourse, 32–3
craftsmanship, 10, 20, 27; industry differs from, 33; morality of, 64–6; Morris's view of, 31; tradition and, 56
cross (the), 8–9, 10; typological connotation of, 10, 24; *see also* ornament
cross-axial composition, 58–9
cross axis, xiv, 59
Crown Hall, 78
Crystal Palace, 17, 85
Cubism, 44, 87
cultural commodification, 76, 78
cultural experience, 28
cultural products: reification of, 78
cultural secularization, xiii, 9, 20; montage and, 26–7; poetic dimension of, 45

culture: bourgeois, 54; and civilization, 52, 53; nature and, 32; and technology, 48–9, 69
culture of building, 38, 39, 41, 54; construction of new typologies from fragments of, 46
culture industry, 54, 69, 82, 108n28

Dadaism, 44, 87
Dal Co, Francesco, 76
Damisch, Hubert, 17, 73
David, J. L., *The Death of Marat*, 15
"death of architecture," 4, 52–3, 54, 90
death of the author, 94n54
death of subject, 19, 94n54
deconstructivist architecture, 20, 87, 89
decoration, 24
decorative (the): concept of, 109n31
Deleuze, Gilles, 26, 96n76, 106n23, 109n32; on minor language, 68, 78, 106n23
design, 35; and building, 16; and construction, 2–3, 6; lineaments in, 7; mechanization of, 14; separate from structure, 9
design economy: of Mies van der Rohe, 68, 69, 70–2, 73; of Wright, 58–9, 64
De Stijl, 43, 75, 86
detail, 18, 40
"dialectical image" (idea of), 43, 45–6
dis-joint, 3, 27, 90
distanciation, 27–8
Doesburg, Theo Van, *Russian Dance*, 70
Dom-i-no, 36, 37, 53; *see also* Le Corbusier
dressing (*Bekleidung*), 22–3, 64, 88; in Loos, 49, 50–2; Semper's theory of, 23–4, 57; in Wright, 58, 66–7; *see also Bekleidung;* clothing; weaving
duality, 2–3; of body and matter, 8–9; of form and construction, 16–17
Durand, J. L. N., 13–14, 15, 37, 38, 81

INDEX

dwelling, 26, 78, 84, 85; aura of, 56; culture of, 76; ethos of, 67; secularization of, 98n24; *see also* Heidegger, Martin
dwelling tradition, 43, 44; of Wright, 56–67

earthwork (the), xii, 20, 78, 90; relation with framework, 17
eclecticism, 2, 58, 66
Ecole des Ponts et Chaussées, 5
Eisenman, Peter, 36
Ekenäs Savings Bank, 105n18
Eliot, T. S., 56
enclosure, 20, 21, 24, 87; masonry, 64; in Mies van der Rohe, 77, 79–80; in Wright's plan, 62, 64
engineering, 5, 6, 36, 37, 38
English domestic architecture, 98n23
English picturesque architecture, 56
epistem, 14
Eupalinos (Valéry), 39
experience: automization of, 1; concept of, 54

fabric, architecture as, 27
fabrication, xiv, 2, 10, 24, 28, 86; concept of, 5; dialectic understanding of, 27; integration of beauty with rules of, 12; technique in, 29
fabrication process, 13
facade, 38, 50–2, 53; free, 54; of Loos's houses, 46–7
Farnsworth House, 76
festive structures, 24, 25f
50 × 50 House, 76–7, 77f
figurative representation, xii, 37
firmitas, see Vitruvian triad
Florida Southern College, 66
form(s), 7, 15, 27, 40–1; atectonic/tectonic, 23; classical, 82; classification of, 13; and construction, 16–17; as expressive element, 2; and its tectonic figuration, 66; meaning inherent in, 14; metaphoric operation of, 46; structural rationality and, 64; and structure, 77; and technique, 53; technological/architectural, 39

formalism, 35
Foucault, Michel, xii, 11, 14, 73, 81, 94n54
fragmentation, 3, 19, 27, 90
framework, 20, 78, 90; relation with earthwork, 17
Frampton, Kenneth, 17, 19, 24, 53, 54, 86
Franciscono, Marcel, 33
Frankfurt school, xi
Frascari, Marco, 24
Freud, Sigmund: *Civilization and Its Discontents,* 108n28
functional rationalists, 73
Furness, Frank, 2

Gadamer, Hans-Georg, 88
Galileo, 5, 12, 14
Gaudi, Antonio, xiii
German realist architecture, 98n23
Germany, 30, 31, 35
Giorgio, Francesco di, 10
Gothic architecture, 1–2, 17
Gothic revival, 29–30
grand narrative, 90, 94n54
Gravagnuolo, Benedetto, 45–6
gravity, 7, 40, 66, 73
Great Exhibition of 1851, xi
Greco-Gothic architecture, synthesis of, 23
Greek architecture, 21, 24
Gregotti, Vittorio, 82, 89
Gropius, Walter, 30, 31–2, 33–4, 38, 39, 41; Georgian window, 33–4; "Gropius at Twenty-Six," 32; *Scope of Total Architecture,* 32; understanding of the artifact, 35–6
Guardini, Romano, xii, 106n22
Guattari, Félix, 26, 96n76, 106n23
Guggenheim Museum, 67
guild system, 5, 9, 30

Handwerk, 32–3
Hartlaub, G. F., 35
Hays, Michael, 105n21
hearth, xii, 20–1, 22, 26, 58, 59, 85; as center, xiv; emphasis on, in Wright, 61, 66–7
Heidegger, Martin, xii, 2, 40, 77, 88, 109n30; on beginning, 54, 88; on dwelling, 84; on "event," 107n15

Hilberseimer, Ludwig, 106n21
Heller, Agnes, 11
Herrmann, Wolfgang, 23, 85
hermeneutics of suspicion, 27, 69
heterotopia, of Wright's architec-
    ture, 62–4, 67
"heterotopic" language, 58
historical avant-garde, 87; in archi-
    tecture of Mies van der Rohe,
    68–70
historicism, xiii, 3, 29–30, 34, 43,
    54, 56, 57, 68, 85, 90, 104n29;
    transcending limits of, 20
history, 7, 41, 42, 69, 81–2
Horner House, 54
Horta, Victor, 2
house: ethos of, 47–8; of Loos,
    xiii–xiv
House for a Bachelor, 73, 74–5
"house-machine," 37
Hubsch, Heinrich, 25
human existence: in/and architec-
    tural discourse, 86–7
humanist discourse, 1, 22, 89
hut, 21; basic structure of architec-
    ture, 14, 85; Great Exhibition,
    London, 21f; see also Caribbean
    hut; Laugier, Marc-Antoine

Illinois Institute of Technology,
    78, 79f
industrial arts, 20–1
industrial materials and
    techniques, 1–3
Industrial Revolution, xi
industrial work, alienation of, 32
industrialization, 94n56
industry(ies), 31, 36; different
    from craftsmanship, 33; inter-
    communication between, 24–5
inside/outside, 15, 22; in Loos, 48,
    54; in Mies van der Rohe, 75,
    80; simultaneity of, 89; in
    Wright, 62
intention, and construction, 27
interiors, 49–50; of Loos's houses,
    xiii, 44, 46, 47, 49–50, 52, 54
international style, 57, 58, 66,
    104n29

Jameson, Fredric, 94n54
Johnson Wax Building, 66
joinery, 25–6, 85

joint, xv; function of, 27; import
    of, for the tectonic, 17, 18, 24;
    knot as primordial, xii

Kahn, Louis, 42, 82, 86, 90
Kandinsky, Wassily, 76
Kelly, Smith Norris, 57, 58
Kent House, 61, 61f
Klee, Paul, 44–5, 84
knot, xii, 24, 25f
Kosmos, xv, 88

language: problematization of,
    106n23; truth content of, 88; see
    also architectural language
Laugier, Marc-Antoine, 1, 2, 16,
    85; Essay on Architecture, An,
    82–4, 83f; hut, 14, 16, 31,
    82–4
Leçons d'architecture (Durand),
    92n30
Le Corbusier, xii, 2, 30, 38, 39,
    41, 59, 76, 87; and new building
    technology, 53–4; piloti, 90; To-
    wards a New Architecture, 36, 43,
    view of "new objectivity," 36,
    37–8; white architecture, 22–3;
    see also Dom-i-no
Ledoux, Claude-Nicolas, 93n39
Levine, Neil, 82
life-world, xiii, 90
lineaments, 50; see also Alberti,
    Leon Battista
loggia, 50, 53–4
logocentrism, 20
logos of making, 13, 40, 50; techne
    as, 10–12, 29
Loos, Adolf, xii, 30, 39, 43–55,
    45f, 47f, 49f, 90; "Architecture,"
    52–3, 57; and Das Andere, 30;
    idea of dressing, 64; interiors,
    xiii, 44, 46, 47, 49–50, 52, 54,
    87; on ornament, 9; position in
    history of contemporary archi-
    tecture, 4; Prinzip der Beklei-
    dung, Das, 22; Raumplan, 50, 53,
    54; and tomb, xiii, 4, 45
Looshaus, 45–6, 45f, 47f, 48f

machine (the), 31, 32–3, 35; archi-
    tecture and, 36, 76; as new met-
    aphor, 37; Parthenon as, 99n32;
    in poetics of architecture, 64

machinery, 36
Maison Planix, 53
"making": concept of, 1; see also logos of making
Malevich, Kasimir, 77, 109n33; White on White, 77
Mallgrave, Harry Francis, 94n56, 95n60, 98n23
man-made environment, structuring of reality of, xi–xii
marble, 46, 76
Martin House, 62, 62f
Marx, Karl, 9
mass consumption, xi, 36
mass-media technology, 20, 87
mass production, 41
material(s), 3, 7, 11, 13; form and, 41; metaphoric operation of, 46; new, 30, 37, 39, 53, 58, 94n56, 98n23; physical rules covering, 7; relation with structural efficiency, 14; traditional, 56; use by Wright, 62, 64–6
meaning: and construction, 1; inherent in form, 14; work and, 5, 12, 13
means–end relationship, 84
mechanical arts, 5–6
mechanical sciences, 6
mechanization, 9, 29, 56; of design, 14; impact on art, 101n13
mechanization of production/reproduction, 1–2, 3, 19, 33
memory, 41, 46
métier, 56–7
Metropolis, xiii, 19, 67; individual in, 48–9; spatial organization of, 48–9
Michaelerplatz, 46
Mies van der Rohe, Ludwig, xii, xiv, 3, 68–80, 71f, 72f, 74f, 75f, 79f, 87; "less is more," 73; planimetric organization of, 70–2, 74
Miesian motif, 74, 75–6
Miesian tectonic, 90
modern age, 12–13, 27
modern architecutre, 43–55; tradition and, 82–3
Modern movement, 31, 39, 41, 43, 57; schools of thought in, 34–5

modernism, modernists, 6, 16, 20
modernity, xv, 1–2, 56, 68; Baudelaire on, 81; montage in, xiv; and tradition, 44–5, 54, 55, 66
moderns, ancients and, 44, 81–2
Moller House, 53
montage, xiv, 1, 5–28, 45, 89; importance of, 3; Loos's use of, 46–9, 54–5; in Mies van der Rohe, 78–80; poetic task of, 28; and secularization of cultural production, 26–7; and sewing, 26; visual, in arcades, 44; in Wright, 58, 64
monument, xiii, 45, 89; as event, 4; as ornament par excellence, xv; see also Semper Gottfried; Vattimo, Gianni
monumentality of architecture, 88–9
Moos, Stanislaus von, 36, 53
moral functionalists, 6
moral issues, in architeictural production, 18
Morris, William, xi, 31, 32, 98nn23, 24; "Revival of Architecture, The," 29–30
Mumford, Lewis, 104n29
Museum of Modern Art (New York), 57–8
music, xii, 3, 88
Muthesius, Hermann, 35, 41; sociopolitical project of, 98n24

naturalism, 34
nature, 12–13, 57, 84, 86; and civilization, 99n36; and culture, 32; modern attitude toward, 37–8
neo-avant-gardism, 20
Neue Sachlichkeit, 35
Neumeyer, Fritz, 100n4
new (the), 20, 78, 82
New National Gallery, 78
"new nature," 44–5
new objectivity, 30, 39, 41; spirit of time and, 34–8; see also Neue Sachlichkeit
Newton, Sir Isaac, 15
Nietzsche, Friedrich, 9, 109n30
nihilism, 9; of Loos, xiii, xiv, 54; of technology, 4, 76, 78, 90
novel, 19, 28

object: and its representation, 77; shift in interest from, to process, 13; subject and, 69

object type(s), 36, 39, 41, 78; and logos of making, 40; real use of, 38–9

objectivity, 36–7, 38; formal, 35; see also new objectivity

objets d'art, 39

ontology of architecture, 82–90

ontology of the present, xiv, 81, 85–6, 87

open plan, 38, 77; see also plan libre

order, 10–11; in Mies van der Rohe, 69; as theme in classical discourse, 11; in Wright's architecture, 61

ornament, 39; and beauty, 105n10; body of Christ as, 8–9; column as, 72–3; construction and, 16; monument as, 89; as necessity, 40; position of, 17, 18; and structure, xv, 2, 88; in Viollet-le-Duc, 24, see also cross

ornamentation, and construction, 18

painting, xii, 37–8; abstract, 109n33

Palazzo Rucellai, 7–8, 8f

Palladio, Andrea, 6, 11–12; Four Books of Architecture, The, 10

Paris, 5

Parthenon, 99n32

Paxton, John, 17

perception, 81

Pérez-Gómez, Alberto, 81, 84, 91n3

Perrault, Claude, 13, 14–15, 81

Perret, August, 57

Peruzzi, Baldassare, 49, 50, 51f

Pevsner, Nikolaus, 31

Piranesi, Giovanni Battista, 80, 81, 86

place: archaic sense of, 61; being and, 58, 59; and production and architecture, 86; sense of, 59, 62

place-form, 86

plan-libre, 53, 54; see also open plan

plastic sensibility, of Mies van der Rohe, 70; in Wright, 64–6

Poelzig, Hans, 39

poetics: of architecture, 64; of technology, 38–42

Porphyrios, Demetri, 46, 105n18, 107n12

positivism, 31–2, 37, 41, 91n3

postfunctionalism, 89

postfunctionalist architecture, 68, 78

postmodern architectural discourse, 87–8, 94n54

postmodern architecture, 4, 87, 110n33

postmodernism, 89; simulation of historical forms, 80

postmodernity, 68

poststructuralist discourse, Semper in, 19–23

practice, theory and, 2, 6

practical arts, 85

Prairie architecture, xiv, 58–9, 67

preindustrial civilizations, xii, 48

Pre-Raphaelites, xi

present (the): past and, 43, 45, 56

Price, Bruce, 61, 61f

private/public space, 44, 50

process, 13; imperative of technology, 30–4

production: mechanization of, 1–2, 3, 19, 33; mode of, 88; and place and architecture, 86; in Semper, 24–5

production line, 30, 43, 86

progress, 3, 30, 42, 45

project, idea of, 87

projection, 84

Pugin, A. W. N., xi, 18

Queen Anne style, xiii, 56

railroad stations, 44

Rajchman, John, 106n4

realism, 98n19, 100n35

realist architecture, 57, 90, 103n7

reality, 94n54

Red House, 56

regionalism, 67, 98n24, 104n29

regulating line (the), 59

Renaissance, 11, 15, 49, 73, 90

Renaissance architects, 2, 7–8

Renaissance architecture, 22, 24

Renaissance culture, 8, 10

representation, 39, 50; construction and, 3; constructive

components of existence in, 84; problem of, 82–4

resemblance, 10, 11, 72

Richardson, H. H., 102n16; domestic manner, xiii

Ricoeur, Paul, 28, 69

Rietveld, Gerrit, 86

Robie House, 59, 60f, 61

Rococo architecture, 70

Roman architecture, 50

Romantic movement, 29

roof, 20–1, 37, 40, 58, 85; see also Wright, Frank Lloyd 59–61, 64, 66–7

roofwork, xii

Rousseau, Henri, 32, 44

Rowe, Colin, 68

Ruskin, John, xi, 2, 17, 94n48; Seven Lamps of Architecture, 18

Russian Constructivists, 6

Russian Dance (artwork), 70

Rykwert, Joseph, 81

Sachlichkeit, 34–5, 98n23

Said, Edward, 96n78

Saint-Simon, Claude-Henri de, 32

Santa Maria del Fiore, 5

Sartre, Jean-Paul, xii

Scarpa, Carlo, xiv–xv

Scarry, Elaine, 9

Schinkel, Karl Friedrich, xiii, 50, 51f

Schlemmer, Oskar, 31f

Schmalenbach, Fritz, 35

Schroder-Schrader House, 86

Scope of Total Architecture (Gropius), 32

Seagram Building, 78

Secessionism, Secessionists, 30, 52, 53

secularization, 3, 4, 32, 54, 95n56, 102n19; of architectural production, 16, 28; of architecture, 54; of context of the life-world, 87–8; destiny of, 109n30; of dwelling, 98n24; historical progression of, 26–7; of language of architecture, 69; liquidation of traditional values in, 56; of metaphysical context of the tectonic, 89; radicalizing, 109n31; of spiritual values, 48; undermining classical thought,

12–13, 16; see also cultural secularization

secularization of construction (theme), 1, 3–4, 9, 90

semblance, 107n7

Semper, Gottfried, xi, xii–xiii, xv, 7, 21f, 25f, 27, 52, 57, 58, 64, 89; and architectural realism, 110n35; Caribbean hut, xi–xii, 85; earthwork–framework relationship in, 17; generic structure of thought in, 24–5; influence on Wright, 66; on monument, 89; on origin of architecture, 85–6; roof in, 60; Science, Industry, and Art, xi, 19–20; Stoffwechsel, 85; tectonic of, 1, 3, 18, 19–23, 78, 88, 98n23, 107n12; on theatricality, 89, 109n33; weaving, 20; wickerwork, 21; see also hearth

sense perception, 96n76

settlement, 67, 84

Seven Lamps of Architecture (Ruskin), 18

sign: distanced from signifier, 27–8; and signifier, 3

signification: construction and, 16–28; process of, 24; in Wright, 67

signified (the), 6–7; sign and, 3; sign distanced from, 27–8

similitude, 11, 72

Simmel, Georg, xii, xiii

simulation, 94n54

sociology, and architecture, 32

Sola-Morales Rubio, Ignasi de, 109n32

soul, body and, 15

space: covering, 23; dialectical relationship between perceived, conceived, and lived, 26; interior, 52, 53; mathematical distribution of, 50; painting as, 38; private/public, 44, 50; purposeful, 3

space making, tectonic of, 88

spatial displacement, 53

spatial organization, 53; in Mies van der Rohe, 70, 79–80

spatial practice, 26

spatiality, 88; in Semper, 19, 20

sphere, 15

spirit of time, 43; and new objectivity, 34–8; *see also Zeitgeist*
stair, 38; in Loos, 53
steel and glass, 17, 69, 76
Steiner House, 44, 46–7, 50, 52, 53, 54; montage in, 49–50, 49f
storytelling, 19, 28
Streiter, Richard, 98nn23, 24, 103n7
structural efficiency, material and, 14
structural order, 73, 75
structural-symbolic (the), 23–4, 27
structure: and appearance, 7–8; in architectural theory, 90; corporeal nature of, 73; design separate from, 9; form and, 77; and ornament, xv, 2, 88
style, 7, 16; as choice relating to essence of a building, 14; and construction, 5, 6; in nineteenth century, 18, 26
subject: death of, 19, 94n54; and object, 69
surface, 24, 38; see also clothing; dressing
Surrealism, 87
symbolic function of architecture, xv, 13, 18, 88–9
symbolism, 89
symmetry, 11, 12, 13, 26, 34
Synthetic Cubism, 77

Tafuri, Manfredo, 91n3, 104n4
techne, 1, 2, 26, 39–41; in classical thought, 10–11; defined, 2; as logos of making, 10–12; poetics of classical wisdom, 5–16; replaced by technique, 29; replaced by technology, 13; in Vitruvius, 84
technique, 28, 29, 105n21; art and, 32; form and, 53; liquidation of language of art by, 76; new, 37, 39, 53, 98n23; traditional, 56
technology, xi, xiv, 3, 4, 35–6, 40, 53; architecture and question of, 29–42; art and, 33–4, 36, 39, 43, 76, 105n21; change in, 87; and culture, xi, 48–9, 69; and culture of dwelling, 76; effect on architecture, 6, 33–4, 76–7,

78; in modernism, 16; and moral values, 30; nihilism of, 4, 76, 78, 90; poetics of, 38–42; process as imperative of, 30–4; redemptive focus of, 9; replacing *techne*, 13; and tradition, xiii
"technostatic experience," 25, 26
tectonic (the), 7, 16–28; concept of, 16–17; demythification of construction and, 90; meaning of, 40–2; metaphysical context of, 89; as raison d'être of classical architecture, 107n12; recoding, 5–28; Semper's thought on, xii, 1, 3, 88
tectonic figuration(s), 88, 89, 90; of Wright, 64–6
tectonic form, montage in, 27
textile industry, xii, 3, 25–6, 85
theory, and practice, 2, 6
theory of architecture, tectonic in, 18–19
three-part composition (principle), 2, 12, 27
Tigerman, Stanley, 68
tradition, xi, xiv, 16, 86; in Arts and Crafts movement, 56; awakening moments of, in modern architecture, 43–55; and civilization, 67, 87–8; the classical in, 83; devaluation of, 78; mechanization and, 33; modernity and, 44–5, 54, 55, 66; moral values of, 30; possibility of genuine experience of, 19; and present architectural practice, 82–3; restatement of, with new means and materials, 42; and technology, xiii; transfer of, 3; in Wright's architecture, 66; 67, *see also* dwelling tradition
truth, construction as criterion of, 76
Tugendhat House, 72, 73, 74, 74f
type, 40, 41–2; construction and, 10–11, 13
type-tectonic, concept of, 41–2
typology(ies): in Loos, 52–3, 54; new, 46
Tzara House, 53–4
Tzonis, Alexander, 14

INDEX

Unitarian Church, 66
unity, 11; in architecture, 2, 12; of
    work and meaning, 10, 13
Unity Temple, 64, 65f
urban life, 44, 45
Urban Residence project, 50, 51f
utilitas, see Vitruvian triad
utopia, 4

Valéry, Paul: Eupalinos, 39
values, 2, 4, 87; and construction,
    1; decomposition of, by Mies van
    der Rohe, 69; of guild system, 9
Van de Veld, Henry, 57
Vattimo, Gianni, xii, xiii, 3, 28,
    54, 89, 102n19, 109n30; *Verwin-
    dung,* 109n30; *see also* seculariza-
    tion; weak thought
Venetian ducal palace, 18
Venturi, Robert, 68
venustas, see Vitruvian triad
vernacular tradition: in Loos, 57;
    in Wright, 58, 62
Vico, Giambattista, 66
Vidler, Anthony, 15–16
Villa Farnesina, 49, 50, 51f
Villa Savoye, 38
Villa Stein, 53–4
Villari, Sergio, 93n39
villas, Palladian, 10, 11–12
Viollet-le-Duc, Eugène, xiii, 2,
    16–17, 18–19, 23; "Architecture
    in the Nineteenth Century –
    Importance of Method,"
    29–30; *Entretiens,* 34; positivism
    of, 24; structuralist thinking of,
    16–17, 18
Vitruvian triad, xii, 2, 7, 27
Vitruvius, 1, 10–11, 17, 89; archi-
    tectural discourse of, 29, 84–5,

86; *De Architectura,* 2, 6–7; unity
    of architecture in, 12

Wagner, Otto, 95n60, 98n23;
    *Sketches, Projects and Executed
    Buildings,* 98n19
wall(s), 6, 13, 23, 37, 38, 40, 50, 85,
    86; genealogy of, 68–80; mean-
    ing of, 22; in Mies van der Rohe,
    70, 71–6; in Renaissance, 11; in
    Semper, 21–2; structural func-
    tion of, 23–4; in Wright, 61, 62
Ward Willitts house, xiv, 58–9,
    59f, 61, 64
weak thought, xii, 54, 55, 102n19
weaving, 20
Webb, Philip, 56
Werkbund school, 6, 30, 32, 35,
    36, 39
whole–parts relationship,
    16–17, 27
Wigley, Mark, 22
Winslow House, 62–4, 63f
Wölfflin, Heinrich, 34
work: in classical thought, 6–7,
    10, 11; cultural typologies in,
    10; and meaning, 5, 12, 13
Wright, Frank Lloyd, xii, xiv, 59f,
    60f, 62f, 63f, 65f, 70; aesthetic
    valorization of, 62, 64; disman-
    tling of classical composition,
    61–2; planimetric organization
    of, 58, 61–2; the roof in, 59–61,
    64, 66–7; dwelling, 56–67; tri-
    partite compositional order, 62–4

Yourcenar, Marguerite, 108n21

Zeitgeist, 52, 66, 69, 87; *see also*
    spirit of time